—— THE ——
MYSTERY
of

2nd Edition

D1609532

**"An In-Depth and Electrifying
Message of End-Time Prophecy"**

RICHARD GLENN

The late Cato Weatherspoon, II, who helped instill the fear of God in me as a teenager through his fiery preaching.

To the aged servants of God, many years past, at the Zion Congregational Church of God in Christ (better known as Mack Ave.), whose wise words in "Y.P.W.W." and Sunday School didn't return to God void but accomplished what He pleased in the youthful ears that heard them.

The late Dr. Morris Cerullo, God's servant, the chosen warrior, a general in God's Victorious Army, whose powerful teachings I have been privileged to witness since 1973, has been a great help and inspiration. I love him very much.

The late Charles Finney, though he went to glory many decades ago, and I never personally met him, I feel that I know him for his ink and pen of many years past that are yet anointed and affecting the children of men.

Connie McCollum, who was instrumental in helping me when I first started writing.

My good friend, Pastor Salara Mann, of Harrisburg, Pennsylvania.

To Dr. Gertrude Stacks, a great woman of God who is the Pastor of Shalom Fellowship International in Detroit, Michigan.

To my fellow prayer partners, the original "Spiritual Hitmen," Pastor Melvin Walker, Elder Dino Allen, Elder Dennis Rudolph,

Brother Frank Hoskin, Anthony Jacobs, and Corey Jackson (the 133rd Psalms of David).

My good friend, Elder Larry Wilson, who was there when the Spirit of God anointed me and gave me boldness to preach His Gospel while we were both students in college in the early nineteen seventies.

My sister, Beverly Glenn, a pioneer of contemporary gospel music. One of the great composers of this generation. Thanks, Bev, for all your help.

The late Pastor V.B. Washington, who preached the message that stirred me to come to the altar while he was a guest speaker at my church in September 1970.

To the late Dr. Noah Hutching and his wonderful end-time prophecy radio broadcast in the 1970s and 1980s titled "The Watchmen on The Wall." To the late Dr. Hal Lindsey, the great end-time prophecy author. To another great end-time prophecy author, the late Dr. Salem Kirbin.

And last, but not least, to Anne and our children: Dania (Tricie), Charity, Cherie, Timothy, JoAnna (Nicki), and Faith.

I commend all of you as I write this book to the glory of God.

DEDICATION

———— ༄༅༆ ————

To Timothy Richard Bernard Glenn, my Beloved son and friend. "O Timothy, keep that which is committed to thy trust. Carry the legacy baton forward, stand in the gate of the House of the Lord in this last hour. Preach and teach the Gospel of Jesus Christ with all your heart!" II Timothy 1:1-2, Jeremiah 7:2, I Timothy 1:18, II Timothy 4:1-5.

INTRODUCTION

—— ୬୬୨୧ ——

O ne day in the near future, many millions of Christians will suddenly vanish from the face of this Earth, **"in a moment, in a twinkling of an eye."** This will be followed by great confusion, for there will be reports all over the globe of friends and family members missing without a trace. The Bible warns of this event in the following passages of Scripture:

> *For the Lord Himself shall descend from heaven with a shout, with the voice of the archangel, and with the trump of God: and the dead in Christ shall rise first: then we which are alive and remain shall be caught up together with them in the air: and so shall we ever be with the Lord... Behold, I shew you a mystery; we (Christians) shall not all sleep (die), but we shall be changed. In a moment, in the twinkling of an eye, at the last trump; for the trump shall sound and the dead shall be raised incorruptible, and we (Christians who are alive) shall be changed. For this corruptible (earthly*

body) must put on incorruption, and this mortal must put on immortality... For as the lightning, that lighteneth out of the one part under heaven, shineth unto the other part under heaven; so shall also the Son of Man be in His day... I tell you, in that day there shall be two men in one bed; the one shall be taken (vanish) and the other shall be left. Two women shall be working together, the one shall be taken and the other shall be left. Two men shall be in the field; the one shall be taken and the other left.

I Thessalonians 4:16-17, 1 Corinthians 15:51-53,
St. Luke 17:24 & 34-36

Shortly following this sudden ascension of millions of Christians from Earth to Heaven, an antichrist will arise on the world scene to rule the Earth. He will, at first, step forth on the world stage as a great statesman who will bring solutions to most of the world's problems, including the constant threats of war. This articulate, bright and handsome man will quickly win the hearts of the world through his great acts of diplomacy. He will be loved and admired more than any world political leader in history.

However, the Holy Scriptures reveal to us that shortly after he wins the hearts of the world nations, this man of peace will abruptly change into a man of violence and evil, causing great perplexity and destruction in the Earth for a span of three and a half years. Thankfully, he, along with his diabolical policy, will, at the end of those years, be broken by Jesus Christ as He returns to Earth once more with power and great glory, saving the world from total destruction.

In this book, I will inform and explain why I believe the rapture (the sudden resurrection of Christians from Earth to Heaven) could very well take place in the near future. I will explain why it is possible that the Antichrist could be already alive in the world and his spirit diligently at work in the world behind the scenes, preparing for his sinister policy to be adapted in the Earth.

However, he is hindered, for he cannot step forth to fully adapt his sinister policy in the world as yet; only because of the powerful presence of the Holy Spirit and the saints of the Most High God, who are yet on Earth.

To those of you who are not servants of God, I pray that this book stirs you to receive Jesus Christ as your Lord and Savior. To those of you who are already servants of God, I pray that this study stirs you to seek for a closer walk with the Lord. For within these upcoming pages, you will surely find that "THE MYSTERY OF INIQUITY" is already at work!"

CHAPTER ONE

SIGNS OF THE TIMES

———————— ᴐᑕᴐᑕ ————————

I am writing this book to inform and enlighten you of a subject which is very significant. Particularly because of the day we are living in. I want to expound on a story, a riveting and true story within the pages of past and future history in which the Almighty wants to be told. You and I are living in a mighty time. This writer firmly believes that we are living in a generation where a dispensation could close; Indeed, I truly believe this dispensation could consummate in our day. It will close when:

> *The Lord Himself shall descend from heaven with a shout, with the voice of the archangel, and the trump of God: and the dead in Christ shall rise first: Then we which are alive and remain shall be caught up together with them in the clouds to meet the Lord in the air: and so shall we ever be with the Lord.*
>
> I Thessalonians 4:16-17

the Spirit of God. Beloved, we must not be lackadaisical and lukewarm as those five virgins. For the Spirit of our Lord is daily urging the body of Christ to make haste and fully prepare for His soon return.

The Lord never intended for any of His people to be unprepared and caught by surprise when He returned as those five virgins were. He warned the church in His word:

> *But of the times and the seasons, brethren, ye have no need that I write unto you. For yourselves know perfectly that the day of the Lord (the rapture) so cometh as a thief in the night...But ye, brethren are not in darkness, that that day should over take you as a thief.*

I Thessalonians 5:1-2, 4

The Word of God is telling us that when Jesus returns, He will return as a thief in the night. He will come when people are spiritually sleeping. However, the fourth verse says, "**but ye brethren (the church) are not in darkness as the unbeliever that the Lord's return should catch you by surprise.**" He is coming like a thief in the night to the unbeliever, but not to the servants of God.

We are not supposed to be surprised when the rapture occurs. We are not supposed to be caught off guard. We are not supposed to be sleeping spiritually, as the unbeliever, when Jesus Christ descends from Heaven. But we are to be wide awake and well-prepared when that day arrives. Why? Because we are supposed to know the Holy Scriptures. Although the Scriptures do not tell us the exact time when the rapture will occur, they distinctly reveal to us the season when this great event will take place. That's what Paul meant when he wrote, "But of the times and seasons, brethren, ye have no need that I write unto you." It is not given to us to know the exact day when the rapture will take place. But it has been given to us through the Word of God to know the season. Just like when the leaves on trees begin to turn from green to red or orange, falling off the branches to the ground, followed by cooler temperatures, we take note within our minds that soon, very soon, it will be winter.

In the late winter, when the snow begins to melt away, and the trees start to bud and blossom, the grass starts turning green, and little blades of flowers begin springing up out of the ground, and the geese and robin red breasts suddenly return from the south; then we know that summer could not be very far away, but just around the corner. Why? Because you can see the signs of the seasons.

Well, Beloved, there are signs of the season for the Lord's return. He has revealed those signs throughout the Word of God for His people, so we are not caught off guard. It is God's desire to compel you through the pages of this book that we are definitely in the season of His return.

The unbeliever does not understand these things because they are being guided by the darkness of sin. They are walking around in so much darkness until they can't see what they are stumbling over. Many have the attitude of the grasshopper – he jumps all over the ground, having a wonderful time all summer long. However, he never takes out the important time to prepare himself for winter. He's so happy-go-lucky, jumping and playing, not realizing that soon he will freeze to his death. He doesn't have an instinct within him to understand the signs of the times.

The Pharisees and Sadducees once came to Jesus, trying to tempt Him into showing them a sign from Heaven. Jesus said to them:

> *When it is evening, ye say, it will be fair weather: for the sky is red. And in the morning, you say it will be foul weather today: for the sky is red and has an overcast with gloomy clouds. O ye hypocrites, ye can discern the face of the sky; but can ye not discern the sign of the times?*

St. Luke 12:55-56

There are many people today, not only outside the church but also within, who are in the same frame of mind as those Pharisees and Sadducees. They discern the weather conditions. They can tell ahead of time when it's about to rain. They can tell when it's going to be a beautiful, sunny day because they keep up with the news weather programs. There is nothing wrong with this, but although these people can understand the signs of the weather patterns, they have no discerning and understanding of the signs and seasons of the times in which we are living. They can discern the weather patterns and conditions and prepare themselves accordingly, but they have not taken time to discern the spiritual signs of the times. Therefore, they don't understand that we are living on the very edge of the season for the rapture of the church and the seven years of tribulation spoken of in the Book of Revelation.

The signs of the times are telling the body of Christ we must be very careful that we are not in a state of sleep or slumber when the Lord returns. Jesus Christ warned us to **"take heed to ourselves, lest at any time our hearts are overcharged with surfeiting, drunkenness, and the distractions of this life. So that day doesn't come upon us unawares."** (St. Luke 21:34) He said for as a snare, shall it come on all them (the unbeliever) that dwell on the face of the whole Earth. Then He strongly emphasized, **"Watch (stay awake) ye therefore, and pray always, that ye may be accounted worthy to escape all these things that shall come to pass and to stand before the Son of Man."** (St. Luke 21:36)

Our Lord said *watch*. The word *watch* in the Greek means stay *awake*. We must not fall asleep spiritually. We must not get so wrapped up in the cares of this life until our devotion and consecration to God is neglected. We must, as never before, cling diligently to the instruction of the Word of God. That when the Bridegroom comes, we will have our holy vessels pure and full of anointed oil.

CHAPTER TWO

THE MYSTERY OF INIQUITY

One might ask, "Why do you feel so certain that the second coming of Christ is so nigh? Let's turn our attention to the Book of II Thessalonians, the second chapter, where Apostle Paul recorded a graphic word of prophecy to the children of God.

> *Now we beseech you, brethren by the coming of our Lord Jesus Christ, and by our gathering together unto him, that ye be not soon shaken in mind, or be troubled, by letter as from us, as that the day of Christ is at hand. Let no man deceive you by any means: For that day shall not come, except there be a falling away first, and that man of sin be revealed, the son of perdition: Who opposeth and exalteth himself above all that is called God, or that is worshipped; so that he as God, sitteth in the temple of God, showing himself that he is God. Remember ye not,*

*that when I was yet with you, I told you these things.
And now ye know what withholdeth that he might be
revealed in his time, for the mystery of iniquity doth
already work: only He who now letteth will let until He
be taken out of the way.*

II Thessalonians 2:1-7

I have just shared an important passage of Scripture with you,
which is the very core of this entire book. Let us carefully
examine this profound epistle written by Paul. In this passage of
the Scripture, Paul is prophesying to us of the events which will
take place just prior to and after the Lord's second coming. He
exhorted the church to be vigilant in not allowing false teachings
to deceive them. He stated that before Christ returns, there will
be a great falling away. He mentioned this falling away for the
purpose of letting the church know that when it happens, it will
be a sign that the Lord's return is very near.

Beloved, you and I are living in the midst of the generation of
that falling away right now! A generation where several people
in churches are straying further and further away from the
sound principles and doctrines of Christ. They are beginning to
embrace and conform themselves to the principles of the world
and the doctrines of devils. One does not have to travel very far
in our cities and towns to see how many churches have turned
from sound doctrine to embrace the apostasy of the carnal man.
Many leaders within these sacred buildings as well as lay people

have abandoned and rejected the sound teachings and righteous tutorship of their forefathers and mothers to follow trends of the secular world, mixing those trends in with their worship to God.

They feel you can hold some of the secular world's tenor and style in one hand while clenching the Hand of Christ in the other and yet be called the servant of the Lord. As a result of this mild apostasy and deceiving concept, some have a form of godliness but deny the true power thereof.

Jesus Christ had a strong warning for those within the church who would have this worldly frame of thought. He said,

> *But I have some what against thee, because thou hast left thy first love. Remember therefore from whence thou are fallen, and repent, and do the first works: or else I will come unto thee quickly, and will remove thy candle stick out of his place, except thou repent... "I know thy works," says Jesus, "that thou are neither cold nor hot: I would thou were cold or hot. So then because thou art lukewarm, I will spit you out of my mouth. Because thou sayest, I am rich (in Christ) and increased with goods, and have need of nothing; and knowest not that thou art wretched, and miserable, and poor, and blind, and naked.*

Revelation 2:4-5 and Revelation 3:15-17

devastating position – worse than the great depression of the late nineteen twenties and early nineteen thirties. We are witnessing the contractions of that great economic turmoil that will come right now. These pangs are coming and going, coming with force for a season, then we get relief for a season, but every time these economic contractions return, they are a bit more forceful and more difficult for the world to bear.

When the final contraction comes in the near future, there will be more people unemployed than ever before in world history. Crime will be running rampant as never before because of the vexation of poverty and unemployment. The world will, as never before, be longing for a leader who has the characteristics and abilities to bring forth the solutions.

There will be great trouble also in the Middle East. The great controversy between Arabs and Jews over the Holy Land will seem to have reached the highest boiling point. The threat of all-out war, even nuclear strikes between these nations and the possibility of the entire world getting involved will be at a peak. There will be much perplexity and tension in the Middle East and the entire world. In the midst of the great economic despair and alarms of war, this man of sin will come forth onto the scene. He will come, it seems, from nowhere. He will be one who will have been practically unnoticed in the world, a nobody, but yet will come forth with great brilliance and knowledge. He will have all of the answers to the world's economic and war turbulence. The world will receive this man with open arms because, for decades, they will have been waiting for someone to have the solutions to these great problems. He will be smooth and charming. He will be handsome and crafty. The nations of the world will greatly adore him, eventually electing him as their new world leader.

About two thousand five hundred years ago, Daniel, the Hebrew prophet had a vision about the rise of this Antichrist. He said:

His power shall be mighty, but not by his own power; and he shall prosper, and practice, and shall destroy the mighty (world leaders) and the holy people. And through his policy also he shall cause craft to prosper in his hand; and he shall magnify himself in his heart, and by peace shall destroy many: he shall also stand up against the Prince of princes; but he shall be broken without hand. And the vision of the evening and the morning which was told is true: wherefore shut thou up the vision; for it shall be for many days. And I, Daniel, fainted, and was sick certain days; afterward I rose up, and did the king's business; and I was astonished at the vision, but couldn't understand it.

Daniel 8:24-27

In this great vision, the Prophet Daniel foresaw the enormous political power and influence the Antichrist will possess in the world during the tribulation period. Daniel saw this man with mighty power, a power which will not come from him but from another source. This source of mighty power and influence will originate from the sinister throne room of Hell, where his commander in chief resides.

In the vision, the Prophet Daniel saw that this diabolical man will destroy many people. He saw that he will be very prosperous in the world. He will execute the mighty and the holy people. Daniel saw that this man of sin will magnify himself in his own heart. He will be a proud and arrogant person, lofty and filled with conceit. And the people who live in that day will be under great persecution if they neglect to worship him.

Daniel saw in the vision that this Antichrist will adopt a peace pact in the world. But through this peace pact, he will destroy many people. He also saw that this lawless one will stand up and war against "the Prince of princes." But this Prince of princes will break him, putting an end to his reign of terror. This Prince of princes will be none other than Jesus Christ, who will descend from Heaven, along with all of His holy angelic armies, to destroy the Antichrist and his evil associates in a valley called Armageddon. (I will give more detail on this great battle of Armageddon later on in this book).

After the great vision ended and Daniel recorded it in his script, the Spirit of God told him to shut up and seal the information. God told Daniel this event will not take place in his time. It will be fulfilled in the far distant future. "It will take place in another century many, many years from your time, Daniel." Daniel said he was astonished over the vision, but he couldn't understand what it meant at that time. Now, remember the question we asked, why will the nations of the world allow such a diabolical man to rule over them? They will give him his seat of authority because he will not come on the world scene as a tyrant. He will come on the scene as a brilliant statesman, one who will have answers to most of the world's problems. He will come forth as a great man of peace. He will come forth as the perfect political leader for which the world will have been longing. His charm and good looks will captivate many and as a result, swiftly win the hearts of the nations of the world. However, the world will not realize that this charming, handsome, brilliant, peaceful man, with all of the answers to their problems, will be an evil wolf in sheep's clothing.

Now I want to give you some more details about the part of the vision where Daniel wrote, "by peace this man shall destroy many people." This man of sin will come on the scene as a great peacemaker. He will have the ability to cause great wars and conflicts of nations to cease. As a result of his ability, he will win the hearts of the people around the world. But what did the vision mean when it said by his peace, he shall destroy many?

The Antichrist will somehow come up with a great peace plan which will cause the Arab nations and the Jews' great controversy to come to an end. This evil man will come forth with a peace plan which will stop all war and bickering between Israel and the Palestinians to cease. There will be no controversy between Arabs and Jews in the Middle East. No conflict, no more threat of war, no arguments, no terrorism, and no fighting over land, because the Antichrist's peace plan will somehow appease this great contention. Through his peace pact, somehow, someway, he will cause the Palestinians, Arabs, and Jews to live in harmony. But the Prophet Daniel said this peace will be a false peace. It will come forth and last just long enough to rock the world into a slumber of false security; then afterwards, all hell will break forth. (More on this peace pact of destruction later on in this study).

Now let's take another important look at our core Scripture again in II Thessalonians, the second chapter. This chapter discusses the dangers of the end times concerning the rise of the Antichrist. Apostle Paul recorded an empathetic warning to the body of Christ. He wrote, **"Remember ye not, that when I was yet with you, I told you these things!"** In other words, under the divine inspiration of the Holy Spirit, we are being exhorted to store this significant information up in our hearts and minds. Paul was saying when I was with you, I took out the time to warn you of what's going to take place in the end times. He was implying, don't you forget this vital information, store it up and hide it in your heart. It could save your eternal soul.

I would like to echo those words to those of you who are reading this book right now. Don't you ever forget what the Holy Spirit is informing you within these pages. Always remember what Paul said, "While I was with you, I told you these things." For centuries, several biblical scholars and theologians have been trying to figure out who this Antichrist will be. Some said Napoleon would be the one. Some said Mussolini. Some said Adolph Hitler would be this man. Others said Joseph Stalin or even Henry Kessinger, but they were all proven wrong. Nobody knows who the Antichrist is because, according to the Scriptures, he hasn't been revealed as yet, and his identity will not be made known until the church is raptured away.

Let's go back to our Scripture text in the second chapter of Thessalonians. There are two verses in this chapter that are extremely important. It reads:

> *And now ye know what withholdeth that he might be revealed in his time. For the mystery of iniquity doth already work: only he who now letteth will let until he be taken out of the way.*

> II Thessalonians 2:6-7

Now I want you to pay close attention to what I'm about to write here because if you miss this, you will not fully understand the core of the message in this study. Apostle Paul wrote, "now you know what withholdeth (the Antichrist) that he might be revealed." Something is withholding or blocking this evil man from being revealed to the world. Something that is having a similar effect as a closed curtain on a stage, blocking and hiding the identity of this lawless one. And that which is covering and blocking his identity is also preventing him from stepping forth on the stage of the world scene.

Paul wrote, "For the mystery of iniquity doth already work." Only he who now letteth will let until he be taken out of the way." What is iniquity? The word iniquity means "lawlessness, treachery, wickedness, a hidden sin." The word mystery means "an unrevealed truth, something that has never been revealed before." The essence of what the Word of God is showing us here is that there is a spirit of lawlessness at work behind the scenes. This great lawlessness is hidden and covered. Its source has not yet been revealed to the world, but it is very much at work behind the curtain of the world, preparing for its time to come. The mystery of iniquity doth already work. He's not going to wait for the tribulation period to get here to start working on setting up his diabolical government. He and his evil colleagues are already working, setting it up now behind the curtain. When his time comes, he won't have to set up and organize his government, for it will be already in place. But the Bible says, **"Only he who now letteth, will let until he be taken out of the way."**

Now in order for us to get a good understanding of this Scripture, we've got to define the word letteth, or let, because if you go by the English definition of this word, you will totally misunderstand what the Spirit of God is trying to show us. The word *letteth* or *let* comes from the Greek word *Katecho* which means to restrain, withhold, to hold back, to hold down, and to hinder. The Word of God said the mystery of iniquity (the spirit of Antichrist) is already working. Only he who now restrains, hinders and holds him back will continue to restrain, hinder and hold him back until "He" be taken out of the way. So, we find that the Antichrist is already at work behind the scenes setting up and preparing for his time of world rulership. But there is another more powerful force working in the world right now restraining, hindering and holding him back from moving forth on the world scene. This "mystery of iniquity," the Antichrist is longing to step forward and begin his reign of terror, but he can't at this time. He can only work behind the scenes in preparation for this time to come. The question is, who is this "He" that is holding back the Antichrist? What is this force which possesses such authority to hinder and block the mystery of iniquity? It is the power of the Holy Ghost!!! The power of the Holy Ghost at work in the world and living inside of the true body of Christ is holding the Antichrist back. There is no other force that could possibly do it. It is the Holy Spirit who has been instructed by Jesus Christ to live within the believers, comforting them, giving them keeping and overcoming power in the world until the Lord returns and takes us away with Him.

seventies and early nineteen eighties, between the Soviet Union and America, there were hundreds of hydrogen warheads being built, not monthly, not weekly, but every single day!

The Russian and Baltic States had in their possession several intercontinental missiles with 100 megaton nuclear warheads. It was difficult to fathom the power which these awesome missiles possessed. But consider this. Just one of these warheads had more destructive power than all of the bombs dropped by all of the armies in the entire length of World War II. If, for instance, just one of these powerful warheads were used over the state of Kansas, everything living in that state would die. People looking in the direction of the blast from as far as 300 miles away would be blinded. And the radiation would continue to destroy people many miles beyond the actual spot of the blast. And Kansas would be totally desolate and unable to inhabit humans for many decades. Back then and currently, despite all of the talk of peace and harmony in Russia, many of these 100 megaton bombs are still in several Russian missile silos aimed at American cities.

I propose to you that one day in the near future after the Antichrist rises to power, he will eventually use some of these powerful weapons of destruction. This alarming statement shouldn't catch the true believer by surprise, for our Lord Jesus Christ warned us that in the last days, man would nearly destroy everything living:

For then shall be great tribulation, such as was not since the beginning of the world to this time, no, nor ever shall be. And except those days should be shortened, there should no flesh be saved: But for the elect sake, those days shall be shortened.

St. Matthew 24:21-22

Right now, you and I are living in a day where mankind has in his possession the power and potential to cause the total extinction of the human race. And during the tribulation period, Satan will cause nuclear strikes in the world so devastating until the Earth will almost be on the brink of total destruction. This is what our Lord was talking about when He said there will be a time of great tribulation, more devastating than any other time since the world began.

Jesus said, "and except those days (the tribulation period) be shortened by His divine intervention, everyone will die." But He will intervene according to the Scriptures, for His elect's sake. He will come and save the world from total destruction by the hand of Satan and the Antichrist. I will share more on this soon coming great tribulation and the Lord's divine intervention later on in this book.

CHAPTER THREE

THE SINISTER PLAN TO MANIPULATE THE HUMAN MIND

———— ༄༅༄ ————

W e are living in a day where tens of millions of people are being messaged and manipulated without their conscious awareness. In North America, along with many other areas of the world, advertisers have been testing and using several methods of subliminal seduction for years as a means to influence consumers' decisions.

The word subliminal means "below the level of consciousness." One of its methods involves the use of extremely provocative stimulus, which persuades people's minds subconsciously by the operation of split-second repetition. In the concept of "subliminal seduction," these advertisers realize that the human mind can conceive information far swifter than the eyes can see.

information in the brain unaware. In effect, the picture ad was so deceptive until practically the only way the hidden message could be revealed was by it being explained step by step to a viewer.

There was another gin advertising ad, which had been used in several other well-known and popular magazines. This ad was also being used on outside billboards in several cities across the country. On this ad, there was a picture of an attractive young woman, neatly clothed in an elegant black dress. This woman was neat from her head to the tips of her fingernails. She had a smile on her face as she was holding a small glass of gin with ice cubes within.

On the left side of the woman was a large container of the gin. Next to it, there was a large glass filled with alcohol, along with some ice cubes and a slice of lime. Once again, as viewers are reading and turning the pages of the popular magazines, glancing at the pictorial ad, they usually saw it as a harmless picture of a business trying to promote their product. Also, when people were driving or walking down a city street taking a glance at the large billboards of this ad, most were not alarmed at all by the picture of this elegantly and neatly dressed woman holding a small glass of gin standing next to a large glass of the same product. However, little did over 90 percent of these viewers realize that deep into the darkness of this ad was a sinister message seeking to persuade individuals to engage in sinful activities. In the large bottle next to this woman hid from the conscious mind was an artistic picture of a woman's genital. Also, in another area of the glass, artistically and subliminally hidden behind the ice cubes and the gin, there stood a naked man. One could see his upper torso, his extremely muscle-bound stomach and his large sex organ. Once again, these hidden pictures were not picked up by the viewers' conscious mind. But as a person glances at the ad for a few seconds or so, he or she could pick up the message of evil in the subconscious mind.

Now, these gin ads which I have mentioned are only a few of hundreds of seductive subliminal pictures being used in most well-known magazines around the world! Many of them having hidden seductive messages are not only geared toward adults and teens but also little children. For one could even find sinister seductive, hidden messages in some children's toy ads as well.

Beloved, can you see what I am seeking to bring to your attention here? I propose to you that the Antichrist will use this powerful and provocative device in an even more diabolical means to influence and captivate the masses of the world to his Satanic policies!

Yes, Beloved, "The mystery of iniquity is already working." The technology of subliminal seduction is so undercovered and deceptive in our society until the vast majority of average people are not even aware of its existence. Yet, it is being used in public advertisement, television, popular magazines, large outdoor billboards, and many other literatures in every single city, in every single hour of every single day. And this writer proposes to you that the day will come when the Antichrist will have complete control of this device, using it to plan sinister subliminal messages like "receive my mark: 666..." "Destroy any who refuse my mark..." "Children, turn in your parents to authorities..." "Parents, turn in your children..." "Execute any who are found reading a Bible or Christian literature..." "Do evil, sin, sin, sin," etc.

The only way a person can be protected from the evil powers of subliminal messages is for that person to be a servant of God and earnestly seeking for the character of Christ. One who is born again and seeking the character of Christ is a person who lives in this world but does not have a desire to partake in its evil activities; An individual who seeks to allow the righteous thoughts of Christ to abide in his or her mind all day long and not the thoughts of Satan.

For example, Isaiah 26:3 says, **"God will keep a person in perfect peace if he keeps his mind stayed on him."** You might ask, do you mean the only thing I can think about 24-hours a day is Jesus? No, that's not what He means. Look at Philippians 4:7-8 for a clearer picture of what God meant in Isaiah 26:3. It reads, **"...and the peace of God, which passes all understanding, shall keep your hearts and minds through Christ Jesus. Finally, Brethren, whatsoever things are true, whatsoever things are** honest, whatsoever things are just, whatsoever things are lovely, whatsoever things are of good report; if there be any virtue, and if there be any praise, think on these things."

The Word of God is showing us here how to be protected from subliminal messages – by keeping our hearts and minds shielded from the evil thought patterns of Satan. This is an example of what Isaiah 26:3 was talking about when it said, keep your mind stayed on God. A child of God keeps his mind stayed on God throughout the day by thinking on God's thought patterns: or thinking the way He thinks. What does God think about? He thinks on truth, honesty, just, purity, lovely, good reports, virtue and praise. He does not think on evil, only righteousness. And God has commanded us in Philippians 4:7-8 to do the same. And as a result, our hearts and minds will be kept and protected through Jesus Christ.

Satan's ultimate plan in the use of subliminal messages is to give the public his evil thought patterns. However, a servant of God, one who is seeking the thought patterns or mind of Christ, would not allow his eyes to dwell on evil television programs, videos, literature—for they understand that one cannot keep God's righteous thoughts in their hearts and minds that way. In short, the only protection individuals can have from subliminal messages is for one to be born again and earnestly seeking the thought patterns of Christ. This desire will help to guard you against being seduced and led astray by Satan's subliminal messages.

There is another powerful form of mind manipulation that Satan uses on a large scale these days, and I want to comment on it. We better be careful about the type of recordings we listen to because the devil is not only using television, motion pictures and popular magazines to subliminally seduce people, but he is also using music like rock and roll, pop, jazz, R&B and rap music. He is even using some so-called Gospel releases more and more to turn many Christians away from "true holiness."

Several Christian recording artists are conforming more and more to the style of the secular world in their songs. In many of these so-called gospel and contemporary Christian songs, it is hard to tell if it's a secular or gospel recording. For the sound, the beat, and in some cases, even the lyrics are similar. And as a result, it's hard to discern the difference.

The Lord God once warned the people of God, **"To make a difference between holy and unholy, clean and unclean."** (Leviticus 10:10) Oh yes, Beloved, the spirit of antichrist is even using music to subliminally seduce and manipulate people into his evil trap.

A composer once stated that "my theology, folk lore and music, especially music – are the unconscious of the storyteller, composer, or musician speaking to the unconscious of the audience, society or culture." In other words, a song writer and musician can use their music as a tool for planting messages into the subconscious mind of the listeners.

It has been discovered that several of these recordings: rock, pop, jazz, rap and even some so-called gospel recordings have evil seductive messages on them when played backwards. As you are listening to these recordings, tapes and CDs, the subconscious mind is picking up and storing the evil messages of lust, lasciviousness, promiscuousness, and rebellion. And the more you listen to these seductive tunes; eventually, the evil spirits within these recordings can be transferred into your spirit and emotions, causing you to indulge in evil activities which you normally would not.

You might not believe this, but it is true. This is one of Satan's most powerful weapons, which he often uses to subliminally seduce and lead many of the young as well as the old astray. And now, in recent years, Satan has caused this sinister device to creep into many so-called gospel songs. It is one of his newest secret weapons to try to subconsciously seduce God's people in an attempt to turn them from the traditions which they've been taught in God's word.

I'd like to ask you a profound question. Are you a slave to invisible messages? Do you find that you crave to listen to rap, pop, jazz, the blues, or the devil's new style of gospel music? If you are, let it go today! For you could very well be under the influence of "the mystery of iniquity!"

CHAPTER FOUR

ARE WE BEING PROBED?

———— ༚༓༚ ————

D o you remember the motion picture and book *1984*, where the people of the Earth were being watched at all times? Well, that fiction book could yet very well someday become a reality. Don't be surprised if "big brother" is in fact, watching you! Many technologies have been invented to keep track of individuals' movements. For instance, years ago, I warned there was a technology that was developed to place a small radio transmitter to a person's body. This transmitter would be able to keep track of every movement of a person. Also, it could be converted to a transceiver that would transmit signals to control the behavior of that person.

There was another device I exposed to my readers in 1994 that made bugging devices obsolete. The government now has a more modern tool of spying. They have a machine that uses a laser beam. Someone with this device could be stationed across the street from your home or apartment and bounce the laser beam off of your window and hear your conversation no matter where you are in that house! Also, if persons sought to have their secret conversations while sitting on a park or street bench, there was a special gun that fired a spike mic into a nearby tree or bush and picks up your complete conversation. Beloved, as of this writing, this technology is available for everyday citizens to purchase and use for spying on others.

I also warned of a device that was being used in many United States cities and still prevalent today. There were motion picture cameras mounted in several strategic locations which have the capability of probing and zooming in on you—taking close-up photographs of people several hundred yards away.

By the way, this device was called "the Big Eye." It is also known that there have been hundreds of powerful satellites which have been launched into outer space for decades. Several of these satellites are highly sophisticated tools. Many are being used daily as instruments of spying, keeping track on countries who could someday pose a threat of hostile intent against our nation. Several of these powerful surveillance satellites are so sophisticated; they can discern a little ball lying on the surface of the Earth. They are so powerful that there is hardly any activity on the earth's surface which they cannot clearly pick up on in a clear view and relay the picture back to the people in control.

One day, in the near future, an evil man will arise to power in the world. And he will take over all of these powerful satellites. He will eventually use them to keep the people of the world under strict surveillance and control.

There are trillions of dollars being spent every year by governments around the world on secret intelligence. In the United States alone, there are over eight intelligence agencies employing countless numbers of people. These agencies have the ability to spy and keep tabs on every single person which they choose in our land. One day the Antichrist will be the commander in chief of all worldwide intelligence. Everyone will be watched, and if you refuse to follow his evil policy by not receiving his mark (666), you will be exiled, placed in concentration camps or executed.

In the near future, no one in this world will be safe even in the comforts of your own home. Have you noticed the rapid rise of cable, satellite and digital television in the last twenty years or so? It is no coincidence it is estimated that over ninety-three percent of homes have some form of cable or digital television. It was the advertiser's desire that one day every single home would have cable. Cable, satellite and digital television are lucrative businesses. Billions of dollars are being made as a result of this big business. Cable and digital television are being advertised as being convenient for families for they don't have to travel to theatres to view their favorite motion pictures. All a person has to do is flick the switch, relax in the comfort of their living room and watch popular and newly released movies.

Christians can sit in their living rooms viewing cable and digital television ministries for hours and receive a touch from God right through the television, phone or computer. People have been divinely healed and saved through some of these digital church services. Truly the consumer market for cable has expanded and spread rapidly across the world. Now, to have cable in a home is as common as having a mobile phone or computer.

Now, please understand, I am not trying to promote nor condemn cable or digital television in your home. But I propose to you that it is highly conceivable that following the rapture of the church, a rising antichrist could use this technology as a means to probe on the privacy of every home in the world. The technology and capability exist where all television sets and remote controls could be converted into sound cameras. If this is so, then it would be possible for an Antichrist to use his intelligence to plug into all cable and digital lines. His intelligence would be capable of sitting in an office and looking into a scanner to see or listen to what your family is doing while the television set is on.

Once again, I would like to say I'm not condemning anyone who has cable or digital television right now, nor am I criticizing cable and digital companies. But I truly believe a day will come where cable and digital television will be used by the Antichrist as one of his means to probe on the people in an attempt to seek out anyone who would dare to oppose his form of government. The day is indeed coming when people are watching the television and "Big Brother" will be watching them.

Many consumers are not aware that several smart devices they are buying and bringing into their homes are capable of making data that can be hacked or collected. Devices like thermostats, cameras, televisions, dishwashers and other household appliances are increasingly connected to the internet and capable of providing ample opportunity for intelligence agencies to spy on targets and possibly the masses.

It is a growing danger in our society in which the spirit of Antichrist is crafting for the purpose of using to probe the people of the world during his evil regime. An intelligence official stated many years ago that "intelligence services will use the internet for identification, surveillance, monitoring location tracking, and recruitment." Police have already started asking some companies for footage of the videos inside homes where the camera was purchased to keep an eye on their children. The potential for "Big Brother" to spy in homes could someday become a clear and present danger. Samsung and other television companies have placed in their products the ability to listen to your conversations in the room where it sits. Also, Xbox Kinect and Amazon's Echo can listen in on your conversations along with General Motor's OnStar program that tracks car owner's driving patterns. Even a barbie doll has the ability to spy on you and your kids. It can listen to you, respond and at the same time send what you say to it back to its creator, Mattel.

One of the most alarming things about these new technology devices being used in countless homes is that many people are not aware that these products can spy on them in their homes or cars. These are only some of many examples showing how the mystery of iniquity is already at work in our society.

Here are some other devices which multitudes of consumers have brought into their homes for conveniences that make it easier for the Antichrist to monitor you in the future: Robotic vacuum cleaners, robotic mops, doorbell cameras, video surveillances and smart refrigerators.

The day is rapidly approaching where Big Brother will be watching each trip you take in your vehicles. The technology is already developed where the present toll booth methods on our highway turnpikes will be soon done away with. Instead, the traveler fees can be calculated and deducted from a prepaid amount by a series of electronic devices that can record your presence, the distance you have traveled, the time and date. The information received is stored automatically into a computer data bank.

Many years ago, the United States government was in the process of spending several millions of dollars for research on the development of a new system called Intelligent Vehicle Highway Systems, or "Smart Roads." This system now uses emerging telecommunications and computer automation technology to manage automobile traffic on the highways and streets.

Another advanced technology of smart roads was (AVI) Automatic Vehicle Identification, or ETTM, Electronic Toll and Traffic Management. Through this technology, drivers placed a tiny tag on their windshields. When their automobile surpasses a special toll lane, a transmitter instantaneously recorded their presence. Also, through special computer systems in other devices, the amount of the traveler's tolls was then subtracted from a prepaid account.

Many years ago, in my first writing, it appeared that the toll industry was gearing toward having these new systems in every major toll road in the U.S. pike systems. Back then, all ten roads of the Oklahoma turn pike systems were already electronically monitoring the travels of over 100,000 turn pike users. Also, the Dallas north tollways were using an identical system to keep tabs on over 40,000 regular commuters on their 15-mile stretch. Beloved, can you imagine what it will be like when all highways have this system in place, monitoring all highway destinations and whereabouts?

It even gets more alarming than this. At a well-known institute of technology, a multi-million-dollar program was adapted to study and develop smart road technologies. They foresaw the possibility of eventually adapting "congestive pricing," which will be a day when thousands of electronic tracking devices are placed on all city streets in order to charge all drivers of motor vehicles. This plan was being seriously talked about and will surely be brought forth in the near future.

One can clearly see that a day will come when the Antichrist and his secret agents will not only be able to watch you when you are in your home or taking a stroll on foot, but he will be watching you as you get in your car and travel through the streets and highways. Are we being probed? I'll let you answer the question by filling in the blank. _____!

CHAPTER FIVE

MOVING TOWARD THE MARK OF THE BEAST

―――――――― ჟᲖ ―――――――

Years ago, the government had a system where pay checks would be completely done away with. People would instead receive a credit card, and this card will determine your buying power. As a result of this super credit card, or smart card, money as we knew it would eventually be done away with. Bankers for decades had been seeking to implement a system called Electronic Funds Transfer (EFT). It would allow us to become a cashless society. And they have earnestly sought to move in this direction, envisioning funds being sent swiftly across the world in seconds electronically through a super card instead of cash or checks. My friends, since the first printing of my book, this technology has become our reality.

would not only make information of people and business transactions less complicated, but would also aid in bringing the growing crime rate down because no one will have money or even credit cards, but just a number on their bodies! Now, if you refuse to follow this new system, it will deprive you of doing business transactions or making purchases, because checks, money and credit cards will be obsolete. Does this all sound familiar to you? In the Book of Revelation in the 13th chapter and 16th-18th verses, the Word of God tells us that the day will come when the Antichrist will cause all, both small and great, the rich and poor, the free man and the prisoners to be given a mark on their right hand or on their forehead. And no one would be able to buy or sell except those who have the mark of the beast (666).

I'd like to share with you what I think is a disturbing news article. Some workers in Wisconsin will soon be getting microchips in order to enter the office, log into computers and even buy a snack or two with a swipe of a hand. Todd Westby, the CEO of tech company, Three Square Market, told ABC News today that of the 80 employees at the company's River Falls headquarters, more than 50 agreed to get implants. He said that participation was not required.

The microchip uses Radio Frequency Identification (RFID) technology and was approved by the Food and Drug Administration in 2004. The chip is the size of a grain of rice and will be placed between a thumb and forefinger. Westby said that when his team was approached with the idea, there was some reluctance mixed with excitement. But after further conversations and the sharing of more details, the majority of managers were on board and the company opted to participate with Bio Hax International to get the microchips. Westby said, "The chip is not GPS enabled, does not allow for tracking workers and does not require passwords. There's really nothing to hack in it because it is encrypted just like credit cards. The chances of hacking into it are almost non-existent because it's not connected to the internet," he said. "The only way for somebody to get connectivity to it is to basically chop off your hand."

Three Square Market is footing the bill for the microchips, which cost $300 each, and Westby said that if workers change their minds, the microchip can be removed as if taking out a splinter. He said his wife, young adult children and others will also be getting the microchip. Critics warned that there could be dangers in how the company planned to store, use and protect workers' information.

Adam Levin, the chairman and founder of Cyberscout, which provides identity protection and data risk services, said he would not put a microchip in his body. "Many things start off with best intentions, but sometimes intentions turn," he said. "We've survived thousands of years as a species without being microchipped. Is there any particular need to do it now? Everyone has a decision to make, that is, how much privacy and security are they willing to trade for convenience?"

Jowan Oster Lund of Bio Hax said implanting people was the next step for electronics. "I'm certain that this will be the natural way to add another dimension to our everyday life," he told the Associated Press.

Beloved, I propose to you that this technology's beginning stage is a giant step in the direction of widespread use in all the nations of the world in the not-so-distant future. And a giant step in the direction of moving towards the Book of Revelation's "Mark of the Beast."

The day will soon come where people will need this mark of the beast (Antichrist) in order to deposit or withdraw money from the bank. When they beam the laser beam light on your hand or forehead and there is no number there, then you will be turned away and even possibly put in prison. When you go shopping for food or clothing, or even go to the hospital or clinic for medical care, if you do not have "the mark," you will not be able to receive medical care. What a terrible time that will be.

Beloved, I have been compelled by the Spirit of God to stir you up to the fact that we are literally on the threshold of destiny; we are closer than what many people believe! For the sinister mark of the beast is already prepared to one day be adopted in the world. The reason why you picked up this book was that the Spirit of God has sought to urge you to beware! For the "mystery of iniquity is already working."

CHAPTER SIX

THE RISE OF ROBOTS AND COMPUTERS

W e are living in a generation where robots and computers are playing a significant role in our world—a role that is very much worth paying close attention to by believers. There are computers that have the ability to register a trillion people in a second! There are computers in our world that can give full information on every person in America. There are computers that can give information of a complete stranger's name, age, education, religion, criminal records, profession and much more in seconds just by him giving his name.

Computer technology has indeed made great breakthroughs since the first program-made systems were invented in the 1940s. Before then, people were stuck with using primitive adding machines and slide rule devices. But, oh how things have rapidly changed. Now, these machines are so complex until they have

These robots have size. They can speak, walk, jog, run, and can climb up and down stairs. They can jump over obstacles in front of them and display good balance with the ability to open doors. If by chance you are able to knock them down, they can get back up. If you are able to knock them down three or four times, they continue to get up and continue their advance.

Keep in mind, my friends, the Word of God instills to us that not only will the man of sin have tremendous powers, but he will also have a loyal assistant, the false prophet mentioned in the Book of Revelation, who will possess miraculous powers to do many wonders in the Earth for the Antichrist. His miraculous powers will include causing things that are not human to suddenly come to life and speak words to the people of the world on behalf of the Antichrist. Therefore, it will not be impossible for the Antichrist and false prophet to turn an army of unrefined robots into powerfully sophisticated androids, harkening to their every command marching to terminate any who dare to defy the son of Satan.

I propose to you that the day will come when these robots will practically be impregnable as mighty soldiers for a diabolical Antichrist in pursuit of all who refuse to take the mark of the beast (666). Terminators, I-Robots, or androids might not be as far-fetched as one would think.

Beware people of planet Earth. For the rise of robotic machines and computer technology will one day play a significant role in the Antichrist's sinister plot to govern and dominate the nations of the world.

CHAPTER SEVEN

SCIENTIFIC TAMPERING OF THE HUMAN RACE

S cientific tampering of the human race has been in the minds and hearts of several scientists for many decades now. Indeed, it has been a strong desire of some for a very long time. "We have not yet seen what man can make of man," said B.F. Skinner, behavioral psychologist. In Vance Packard's stirring book, *The People Shapers*, he informed the readers that B.F. Skinner's ringing pronouncement reflects ambition as well as fact. But dramatic efforts are indeed underway to reshape people and their behavior.

Skinner is not alone in his desire, for there are several scientists and human engineers all over the world who share this burning desire and ambition to discover ways to control, modify and manipulate the lives of the human race. They have made great breakthroughs in discoveries in controlling human actions, desires, moods, and thoughts. Many of these scientists are so elated about their breakthroughs until they're almost acting like children waking up on Christmas morning.

One psychologist proclaimed in his elation concerning the breakthroughs: "Never in human history has this occurred before, except in fantasy!" A behavior scientist in a major university called for "a technology of behavior" because "We need to make vast changes in human behavior." Another behavioral engineer said, "We can develop a technology for routinely producing superhuman beings." He said, "We have the technology for installing any behavior we want."

Jose M.R. Decgado, a pioneer in brain probing called for physical control of the mind in order to develop a "pyschocivilized society." He also urged the United States Government to make conquering the mind "a national goal." And yet another scientist stated, "We should reshape our society so that we all would be trained from birth to do what society wants us to do." The statements by these very prominent scientists are enough to run chills up and down our spine. But this is just the tip of the iceberg of what the spirit of the Antichrist is working on behind the scenes in many scientific areas of human tampering and control.

For instance, a psychologist from a very prominent university in America had an amazing breakthrough discovery concerning memory. He discovered through his research that memories of people could be transferred to other individuals. In his theory, this scientist believed that memory molecules not only exist in the mind but also float around anywhere within the body's nervous system, from head to toe. He believed that the central nervous system has few sites where learning is converted into memory molecules and gets pumped out into appropriate areas of the brain during sleep.

Researchers experimented this theory with an inch-long flatworm. The flatworm's brain has over 400 cells. The scientist trained the flatworm's brain to retract into an accordion shape whenever they shined a light in a water tank in which they were placed. Later on, the worms were trained to coil upon the light. Signals were then fed to untrained flatworms. The untrained worms that ate the trained flatworms displayed the exact same behavior when the light was turned on them. Therefore, the memory of the other flatworms was transferred to the cannibal worms.

Later, the scientist tried the theory on hamsters, rats and mice. Rats and mice liked the darkness but were trained to shun darkness by the scientist. Next, the brains of these trained animals were taken out by the researchers and condensed into a soup-like substance and injected into hamsters. After a while, the hamsters began to shun and dislike darkness.

CHAPTER EIGHT

THE RISE OF A FICTITIOUS RELIGION

S omewhere in the world, sitting behind the scenes like a spider hiding in the dark corridors of his mighty web, there is an antichrist. One who knows that his time has not come, as yet, to spring forth and pounce on the people of the world. But he, along with his dark legions of secret agents, are busy at work setting the stage for this demonic government to be unveiled. Then he, along with his multitudes of evil warlords, will march on the world stage to seize all who refuse to follow his policy. His policy will not have to be formed after he rises to power, for it will, after many years of undercover systematic planning, be already in place when his time comes.

Many years ago, I wrote about a new religion on the rise in our world. This religion was literally sweeping across the cities of the nations, claiming tens of millions of followers. It was called "The New Age Movement." This sinister religion is part of the

Antichrist's plan to prepare the world to receive him as their leader when his time comes. I am convinced that the new age movement is the diabolical "one world church," which Apostle John predicted would rise to power in the last days. In the Book of Revelation, the 17th chapter, the sinister church is called *Babylon*, the great mother of harlots and abominations of the Earth. According to Revelation, this church, which will be led by the false prophet, will greatly persecute those who refuse to receive the mark of the beast and conform to their evil doctrine. Revelation 17:3-6 reads:

> *So he carried me away in the spirit into the wilderness: and I saw a woman (the evil "one world church") sit upon a scarlet coloured beast, full of names of blasphemy, having seven heads and ten horns. And the woman was arrayed in purple and scarlet colour, and decked with gold and precious stones and pearls, having a golden cup in her hand full of abominations and filthiness of her fornication. And upon her forehead was a name written, MYSTERY, BABYLON THE GREAT, THE MOTHER OF HARLOTS AND ABOMINATIONS OF THE EARTH (the evil "one world church"). And I saw the woman drunken with the blood of the saints, and with the blood of the martyrs of Jesus: and when I saw her, I wondered with great admiration.*

> Revelation 17:3-6

Who are these saints and martyrs of Jesus? These are two groups of people. The saints will be those who are saved and converted after the rapture and during the tribulation period. They are those who missed the rapture and will pay a great price. The "woman" referenced in Revelation 17 will greatly persecute and kill them because of their stand of not taking the mark of the beast and instead choosing to live for God. By the way, this is evidence that there will be more people saved after the rapture, but they will pay a heavy price as we will discuss later in the study. The martyrs of Jesus will be 144,000 Jews who God will raise up during the tribulation period to preach the Gospel of Jesus throughout the world, causing many to be converted after the rapture. We will speak more on this later in this study.

On December 31, 1986, millions and millions of this new age teachings assembled worldwide in meeting rooms, churches, stadiums and convention halls in a massive attempt to bring in their new age. It was an international meditation day that was organized in sixty nations. As they gathered throughout the world in this meditation, many chanted, calling for their new age messiah to come forth!

These new agers firmly believe that very soon their "christ" or "messiah" will appear upon the Earth. They are convinced that our world is on the threshold of a great spiritual transformation and global crisis, which will soon bring forth an "Age of Aquarius:" which is their new age!

They don't believe Satan is evil. They do not believe there is any sin or evil and they do not believe in a burning Hell. They highly esteem Lucifer as the "bright and morning star" and the "light-bringer." During several of their gatherings, in meditations, many New Agers concentrate their minds on evil phrases "come 666" or "come messiah (Antichrist)" or "come Lucifer."

It is the goal of the New Age Movement to replace all religions with their religion. Many churches have been polluted by this doctrine; some Christian organizations slowly began to compromise, easing up on the truth of sound doctrine in order to allow some New Age teachings to creep into their churches.

The New Age Movement has a great conspiracy. When they convert new disciples in Christian churches, they encourage those new converts to remain in their prospective Christian churches with the purpose of infiltrating those churches and planting seeds to birth out and transform "cosmic Christians." These are individuals who are to bring confusion and seductively promote the sinister New Age doctrine. These new-agers love to nest in churches whose gospel is sugar-coated or watered-down to make the congregation feel good about themselves even when they are not obeying the Word of God. If you are in such a church, my dear friend, beware. For the friendly person who often sits next to you may very well be a new-ager seeking to convert you.

More recently, there is another relatively new and powerful movement on the rise in the land of the United States and spreading all over the world called QAnon. QAnon and its evil spirit spewing out destructive conspiracies full of lies and evil deceptions is causing many thousands to embrace and carry out the cult's diabolical teachings. I firmly believe QAnon is a part of a prerequisite of the mystery of iniquity working in the Earth and playing a role in preparing the world for the Antichrist's eventual walk onto the world stage. I propose to you that these types of cults along with several others on the rise in the world will eventually become devoted followers of the son of Satan and will do anything for him and his cause. I propose to you that these types of cults will even play a role in the capture of all who refuse to take the mark of the beast (666) and turn them in to be imprisoned and executed.

His time has not come as yet, but when it does, the son of Satan will also come on the scene with many lies and deceptions to captivate multitudes all over the world in order to draw them into a diabolical trap in which many will not be able to escape.

Beloved, surely now you can see that "the mystery of iniquity" (the spirit of the Antichrist) is already working. But thank God for His blessed Holy Spirit within the true body of Christ who is hindering, holding back and restraining him until the rapture of God's church takes place.

CHAPTER NINE

THE UNLOCKING OF
THE BOTTOMLESS PIT

Now, let's go back over our foundation Scripture in II Thessalonians. Examining it from verses 7 to 12 "For the mystery of iniquity doth already work: only He (the Holy Spirit) who now letteth (restrain and hold back) will let (restrain and hold back) until He (the Holy Spirit) be taken out of the way (the world).

The spirit of the Antichrist is at work in our world, setting up his sinister government behind the scenes. But he is being restricted in doing everything he wants because of the power of the Holy Spirit. The Antichrist longs to come forth on the world stage, adapting the many evil devices which he and his associates invented. But he must wait because the power of the Holy Spirit is greater than his power. But soon, Jesus Christ will return in the clouds of Heaven. A great trumpet will sound in the spirit world and the dead, who died in Christ will arise from their graves ascending into those clouds of glory. Shortly afterward, we believers who are alive shall be raptured from this Earth to meet Jesus and all the other resurrected believers in the sky and will forever be with the Lord. (I Thessalonians 4:13-18) Afterward, there will be no power in the world to hinder and restrain the workings of Satan and his evil son. After the church is raptured away to glory, literally all of the powers of Hell will break out on planet Earth. Look at Apostle Paul's description of what will take place immediately following the rapture:

> And then shall that wicked one (the Antichrist) be revealed, whom the Lord shall consume with the spirit of his mouth, and shall destroy with the brightness of his coming: Even him (the Antichrist) whose coming is after the working of Satan with all power and signs and lying wonders. And with all deceivableness of unrighteousness in them that perish; because they received not the love of the truth, but had pleasure in unrighteousness.
>
> II Thessalonians 2:8-12

After the Holy Spirit is taken out of this world during the rapture of the church, the Bible says, *"then shall that wicked one, the Antichrist be revealed!"* The Bible says, *"Even him, whose coming will be after the working of Satan."* According to this Scripture, Satan will give his son the Antichrist, all of his abilities to deceive people into unrighteousness.

If you notice, I called the Antichrist Satan's son. Satan is a master copycat. Just like there is a Trinity in Heaven (God the Father, God the Son and God the Holy Spirit), Satan has a trinity. There is Satan (the evil god and the father), the Antichrist (his son) and the false prophet. The false prophet will rise during the tribulation period representing Satan's evil spirit. Just like the Godhead is one, Satan, his son and the false prophet are one. Just like the Holy Trinity sent the Word to become flesh in the world for a season, Satan has sent his son, the Antichrist, from the belly of Hell into the world for a season. Just as Jesus depended upon the powers of the Holy Spirit to perform signs and wonders in the Earth, so too will Satan's son, the Antichrist, lean upon the false prophet to do great wonders and signs in the Earth to try to convince the world that he is the messiah. I will mention more about the false prophet later on in this study.

Apostle Paul wrote further in II Thessalonians that after the Holy Spirit is taken to glory with the church, the Antichrist will use the fullness of Satan's powers and wonders to deceive many in the world. The reason why many will be deceived is that while the church was yet on Earth, they refused to believe the Gospel of Jesus Christ. They refused to repent and turn from a life of sin to follow the ways of God. Many of them made fun of Christianity, making a mockery of the Word of God and the righteous values it stood for. Some felt they had much more important things to do in life than to go to church. Some were once Christians, but they willfully backslid into a life of sin and before they could return to the Lord, the rapture took place. Some plainly didn't believe there was a God.

Therefore, these multitudes of people all over the world will be left behind and will enter into the most devastating seven years that this Earth will have ever known. And because of their refusal to serve the living God when they had the opportunity, multitudes will be under the powerful influence of the Satanic trinity's great deception after the rapture of the church.

However, many of these lost souls will yet have one last chance to be saved, but they will have to pay a mighty price for it (more on this price later).

Apostle Paul also stated that God will allow the Antichrist to send a strong delusion upon many people of the Earth who are left behind. And as a result, they will believe a lie. A lie that will cause great damnation to them during the tribulation period. The Bible doesn't state exactly what this great lie will be, but I believe the Antichrist will deceive the people on Earth into thinking that the rapture was a farce. He will somehow cause the people on Earth to believe the millions of missing people didn't go to Heaven. And he will convince them that he is the true Messiah, not Jesus Christ. And with the technology I have mentioned in earlier chapters, it is not so far-fetched to imagine that the Antichrist could achieve this great worldwide deception after the Holy Spirit and the true church is raptured. This great tribulation period will not be a time of child's play. For literally all of the kingdoms of Hell will be released upon the kingdoms of this world. For Satan knows that his time will be short.

Revelation the 9th chapter says:

> *And the fifth angel sounded, and I saw a star fall from heaven unto the Earth: and to him was given the key of the bottomless pit. And he opened the bottomless pit; and there arose a smoke out of the pit, as the smoke of a great furnace; and the sun and the air were darkened by reason of the smoke of the pit. And there came out of the smoke locusts upon the Earth: and unto them was given power, as the scorpions of the Earth have power.*

Revelation 9:1-3

This was one of several great visions which Apostle John saw while on the island of Patmos. John was put on this desolate and lonely island by Jews because he preached the Gospel of Jesus Christ in their towns. His message was to love not the world neither the things that are in the world, for all that is in the world: the lust of the flesh, the lust of the eyes and the pride of life is not of the Father. He preached, "If you love this world and its evil then the love of God is not in you." And because of this kind of preaching and his stand for Jesus Christ, they put him away on this island in the midst of the sea. But, while he was on this lonely, desolate island, God turned this great misfortune into a glorious victory. For Jesus Christ appeared to him in the realm of the spirit and carried his spirit into the future and showed him the end of time.

John said, "I was in the Spirit on the Lord's day (the tribulation period)" and while he was in the realm of the spirit on the Lord's day, Jesus told John, "I want you to write down and record everything I show you." John's script became the Book of Revelation. Before we finish this book, you will have been informed of many of those mysteries of John's important script, which he recorded under the inspiration of God during the Lord's day.

In this phase of the open vision, John saw an angel, the fifth angel, sounding a mighty trumpet and a star, which was another angel coming down from Heaven unto the Earth. This angel had a key in his possession and used it to unlock an abyss, a pit somewhere on this Earth which has no bottom to it. When this powerful angel opens the bottomless pit, a vast amount of dark smoke will ascend from within the belly of the Earth as the smoke of a great furnace. This dark smoke will be so strong until the sun and the air will be darkened by its eerie presence. As John continued to behold this bleak-looking smoke ascending out of the pit, there came from the midst of this smoke an army of locust upon the Earth. Apostle John recorded the following in his script, "unto them (the locust) was given power, as the scorpions on the Earth have power.

These horrible creatures of Hell were given commandment not to destroy the grass, trees, or crops of the Earth as a natural locust. Instead, they would torment the people of the Earth who missed the rapture and received the mark of the beast (666). They will be told not to kill these people but torment them day and night for five months. The word describes the pain of their torment as the torment of a scorpion when he strikes a man. This pain which they will inflict will be so painful until men will seek to commit suicide. People will run around seeking how to die in order to escape the great torment of these horrible creatures of Hell. But the Bible says death will flee away from them. People will try their best to kill themselves through many different means, but death will not help them to ease the pain.

Can you imagine, Beloved? What kind of creature could possibly be so horrible until men and women would seek for death to rescue them from their presence? As you read on in this 9th chapter of Revelation, the Bible describes what these creatures will look like. It says the shapes of their bodies will look like horses prepared to go into war. On their heads will be crowns like gold. Their faces will look like the face of a man. They will have long hair as the hair of a woman, but their teeth will be sharp and voracious like lions. They will also have mighty wings, which will give a sound like the sound of many chariots and horses running to battle.

The Bible also states that these creatures will have tails with powerful stings on them and they will be given the power to hurt and torment the people of the Earth for five months. Now, I don't know about you, but I don't think I would like to see any of these creatures! John wrote that these locusts would have a king over them who is the angel of the bottomless pit; whose name in the Hebrew tongue is *Abaddon*, but in the Greek tongue, its name is *Apollyon*. If you search out this king, you will find he is none other than Satan himself.

In about 800 B.C., approximately 850 years before Apostle John saw this great vision of the end times, the Hebrew prophet Joel also saw these creatures coming upon the Earth during the tribulation period and he prophesied about them. (Joel 2:4-11) Joel describes them also as creatures with shapes like horses. He said they will run like horses, as John recorded, and their traveling will give a sound like chariots. He wrote they will move on mountain tops and be "like the noise of flames of fire that devour the stubble." They will be as a strong people set in the battle array. Joel recorded that because of these creatures, the people of the Earth will be in much pain. These locusts will run like mighty men climbing walls like men of war. They will be very organized, marching, flying and running together and as a well-trained army will not break their ranks. Joel recorded that they will not fight against one another and they will march in their paths. Also, when a human tries to kill them, they will not die nor be wounded.

The Bible says these locusts "will run to and fro in the city: they shall run up on the wall, they shall climb up upon the houses; they shall enter in at the windows like a thief. The Earth shall quake before them; the heavens shall tremble: the sun and moon shall be dark, and the stars shall withdraw their shining (because of the dark smoke of their presence)." The Word of God also says in Joel the second chapter "this day of the Lord will be great and very terrible; and who will abide it?"

Joel said these creatures will be able to creep upon people's houses and sneak into their windows like a thief. Whenever I read this prophecy in Joel 2, I try to imagine what this horrible event will be like. One day you might be arriving home from work, open your house door, close it and lock it. Your front room might be pitch-dark, so you feel your way to the light switch and flick it on. And to your terror, your front room is full of these horrible creatures who crept into your house while you were away.

Some people will be sound asleep at night in their comfortable bedrooms and all of a sudden, the window will slowly creep up and that sound sleep will turn into a terrible nightmare. This all may sound very scary to many of you, but this is the kind of horror that will take place in all the cities on the Earth after the bottomless pit is opened.

The Scriptures do not tell us how big these locusts will be, but if they are able to sneak into people's windows, we have an idea of their size. And we will also know according to Joel's prophecy that they will be immortal, so no human weapon will be able to destroy them. And we also know, according to Joel's prophecy that they will not be dumb but extremely intelligent.

The unlocking of the bottomless pit of Hell to release these creatures will be only one of twenty-one separate devastating judgements which will come upon the Earth after the rapture of the church. Can you imagine this, Beloved? As horrible as this one penalty will be, there will be twenty others according to the Book of Revelation which those who miss the rapture must endure. I will give detail on the other twenty judgements later on in this book.

CHAPTER TEN

THE RAPTURE

—————⟨ ⟩—————

T he scene was set by the shore of a sea called Galilee. The Master had just recently ascended from Hell after taking the keys of death and Hell from Satan in his very throne room. He had taken those keys and unlocked several prison doors of the Old Testament patriots. When He arose from Hell, He gathered the twelve disciples together for one more important exhortation. He told them He had to go back to Heaven to sit down next to God the Father, but while I'm gone, *"Go ye into all the world and preach the gospel to every creature!"* (St. Mark 16:15) He said, *"You will be witnesses unto me both in Jerusalem and in all Judea, and Samaria, and unto the uttermost parts of the Earth."* (Acts 1:8)

Then a cloud came down and received Jesus taking Him up out of their sight. The Bible says the disciples were looking steadfastly toward Heaven as Jesus departed. Two men (angels) stood by them in white apparel, who also said, *"ye men of Galilee, why stand ye gazing up into heaven. This same Jesus, which is taken up from you into heaven shall come in like manner as ye have seen Him go into heaven."* (Acts 1:10-11) These angels were referring to the rapture, the second coming of Christ (a split second of time when Jesus Christ will return in the clouds of glory with all of His heavenly hosts and resurrect the dead who died servants of God). After they are resurrected, then those of us who are yet alive and are servants of God shall also be lifted out of this world swiftly to meet Christ and all of our spiritual family in the clouds. We all will travel up to the glorious and beautiful kingdom of Heaven to remain in comfort and safety until the end of the seven years of tribulation on Earth.

There are several Scriptures throughout the Old and New Testament which talk about this great event. I'd like to share some of them in this chapter.

> *The voice of my beloved! Behold, he cometh leaping upon the hills. My beloved is like a roe or a young hart: behold, he standeth behind our wall, he looketh forth at the windows, shewing himself through the lattice. My beloved spoke, and said unto me rise up, my love, my fair one, and come away. For, lo, the winter is past the rain is over and gone; the flowers appear on the Earth; the time of the singing of the birds is come, and the voice of the turtle is heard on our land; the fig tree putteth forth her green figs, and the vines with the tender grapes give*

a good smell. Arise, my love, my fair one, and come away!

Song of Solomon 2:8-13

Solomon didn't understand it, but he was writing about the relationship between the church and the Lord throughout the entire Book of The Songs of Solomon. The woman's words in the book represented the church with spiritual love and affection for the Lord. While the male voice throughout Solomon's Song represented the Lord Jesus (the bridegroom) and His love and affection for the church.

In this particular passage, the church is greatly excited because she had heard the Lord's voice. He is coming in a very happy state because He's leaping and skipping. The church's Beloved opened His gracious mouth and said, *"Rise up, my fair (beautiful) one, and come away with me!"* In other words, Jesus will tell the church; you are so beautiful, you are pure, you have washed your robes clean and spotless. You have completely turned from a life of sin to follow me while patiently waiting for my return and you have been faithful to me. You have such a sweet smell (a sweet-smelling savor). You are truly ready, my love. Come and go with me so I can show you to my Father in Heaven. Christ said, *"Lo, the winter and rain is past."* This means the times of bleak trials and tribulations for the church are over. Christ said, now the flowers are appearing and the time of the singing of the birds is come. It's rapture time. It's a very happy and joyful

93

time. It's a time where the birds will be singing, and the church will have joy unspeakable and full of glory. It's rapture time! During this glorious moment, the fig trees will be ripe, putting forth her green figs and the vines with the tender grapes will give a sweet smell. And in the midst of all this, a divine voice will be heard throughout the four corners of the Earth only by the church: *"Arise, my love, my fair one, and come away!"*

In the Book of I Corinthians 15:51-53, Apostle Paul wrote:

> *Behold, I show you a mystery; we shall not all sleep, but we shall be changed. In a moment, in the twinkling of an eye, at the last trump; for the trumpet shall sound, and the dead shall be raised incorruptible, and we shall be changed. For this corruptible must put on incorruption, and this mortal must put on immortality.*

Paul is giving a description of the rapture of the church.

A wonderful part of this mystery is there are some people in this world who will never die. Paul said, *"We shall not all sleep."* This sleep has reference to the death of a child of God. There are multitudes of Christians, whom if they are living when the rapture occurs, will never know what it is to die, for the Lord will resurrect them into the clouds of glory while they are yet alive. Paul said, *"This is a great mystery."* He wrote that this event would take place quickly; as quickly as a person can bat an eye, millions of people will vanish off of the face of the Earth! No, I am not speaking of a myth or a fairy tale. It will surely happen and it will happen very soon. A great trumpet will sound in the spirit world from the heavens. And the dead who died with hope in Christ shall be resurrected into the sky to be with their Beloved Lord and Savior, Jesus Christ. We, who will yet be alive, shall arise after them. As we are lifted into the clouds of glory, immediately, our mortal, frail bodies will be transformed into immortal, glorified bodies with powers and abilities as angels. (St. Matthew 22:30) Paul said, *"For this corruptible (flesh and blood) must put on immortality."* Oh, what an awesome moment that will be: the rapture of the church!

Jesus warned us, *"Behold, I come quickly."* (Revelation 22:12) When He returns at the rapture it will happen so quickly that a person won't have the time to get ready if they're not already prepared. Jesus said,

> *He that is unjust, let him be unjust still: and he which is filthy let him be filthy still: and he that is righteous, let him be righteous still: and he that is holy, let him be holy still.*

> **Revelation 22:11**

In other words, He will return so quickly that whatever state you are in when the rapture takes place, you won't have time to change it. If you are unjust, filthy, unholy, or wicked, you will remain in that state as the rapture happens. However, if you are living a holy, clean, obedient, Christian life, that is the state you will remain during the rapture and throughout all of eternity. That's why the Word of God emphatically emphasizes, *"Seek ye the Lord while He may be found, call ye upon Him while He is near."* (Isaiah 55:6) *"Behold, now is the accepted time; behold now is the day of salvation."* (II Corinthians 6:2)

Jesus said, *"Behold, I come quickly."* The rapture will come and go as quick as lightning. Jesus told us:

> *For as lightning that lighteneth out of the one part under heaven, shineth unto the other part under heaven; so shall also the son of man (Jesus) be in His day..."* I tell *you, in that day there shall be two people in one bed; one shall be taken, and the other left. Two women shall be grinding together; one shall be taken, and the other left.*
>
> St. Luke 17:24 & 34-36

Surely the rapture will happen as quick as an eye blink, as quick as a flash of a lightning bolt in the heavens. So quick until two people will be sleeping in bed, the one who is a servant of God shall vanish and the other who is an unbeliever will remain. Two women will be working together; one will disappear right before the unbeliever's eyes. Two men shall be working on a farm; the believer will disappear, and the unbeliever will remain in the field.

Can you imagine what it will be like all over the world as this event unfolds? Many commercial jet planes will fall from the sky, full of passengers because the pilots who are servants of God shall be caught up in the rapture. There will be mass destruction on the streets and expressways in every city because many Christians will be driving their cars when the rapture takes place. There will be trains derailing, there will be many reports by parents of children missing and a flood of reports by children stating their parents are missing. The world will be full of perplexities because there will hardly be a single-family tree where at least one relative is not reported missing. Apostle Paul wrote:

> *For the Lord Himself shall descend from heaven with a shout, with the voice of the archangel, and with the trump of God: and the dead in Christ shall rise first: then we which are alive and remain shall be caught up together with them in the clouds, to meet the Lord in the air: and so shall we ever be with the Lord. Wherefore comfort one another with these words.*
>
> I Thessalonians 4:16-18

The rapture is soon to come, Beloved. We must be careful that we are not unprepared as the five foolish virgins. (St. Matthew 25:1-3) They were Christians. They accepted Jesus as their Savior. They were church-going people, but they had faults and weaknesses in their character which they were not earnestly seeking to correct. Therefore, when the Lord returned, they were not prepared. *"The door was shut."*

97

We must be careful that we don't be like the servant of God, who received talents from the Lord but wouldn't use them. (St. Matthew 25:14-30) His fellow brothers in Christ also received talents and used them for the furthering of the Gospel, and souls were saved as a result. But the wicked servant was slothful and afraid of what people would think or say if he used his gift, so he sat on it. Then the Lord returned while he was sitting on the talent which God gave him. And the Lord said, *"Thou wicked and slothful servant... And cast ye the unprofitable servant into outer darkness: there shall be weeping and gnashing of teeth."* (St. Matthew 25:30)

One day, as Jesus was sitting on the Mount of Olives, the disciples came unto Him privately and asked, *"...Tell us, when shall these things be? And what shall be the sign of thy coming."* (St. Matthew 24:3) This is a sincere and honest question, an important question, a question which many have asked down through the centuries since the crucifixion and resurrection of Jesus Christ. What will be the signs of the Lord's return? There are several signs mentioned in the Word of God, but I want you to focus on the ones Jesus gave in St. Luke the 21st chapter. Jesus said:

> *And there shall be signs in the sun, and in the moon, and in the stars; and upon the Earth distress of nations with perplexity; the sea and the waves roaring; men's hearts failing them for fear, and for looking after those things*

which are coming on the Earth; for the powers of heaven
shall be shaken. And then shall they see the son of man
(Jesus) coming in a cloud with power and great glory.
And when these things begin to come to pass, then look
up, lift up your heads, for your redemption draweth
nigh.

St. Luke 21:25-28

We are living in a day where every one of these signs which
Jesus predicted would happen in the last days are taking place.
There have truly been several signs in the sun, moon and stars.
Scientists have been examining our sun closely for many years.
There has been a large increase in sunspots. These sunspots,
which look like tiny dots on the sun through our super
telescopes, are actually gigantic storms on this important star.
These storms on the sun's surface are powerful, more powerful
than a hundred atomic explosions combined. Several of these
storms have been spotted in different locations on our sun by
researchers. Some scientists are disturbed about this activity.
They fear that these are signs that our sun is in the early stages
of having a nova. A nova is when a star or sun in the galaxy
either explodes and disintegrates or has an extreme increase in
its heat; then completely blacks out, never to give out heat or
shine again. But prior to a sun's nova, it first goes through this
process of increased solar storms, which our sun has been
experiencing more and more in recent years.

Could it be possible that our sun is in the process of having a nova? What does the Bible say about the sun in the last days? In the Book of Revelation, the Word of God predicts that a day will come when the sun will increase in extreme in heat, tormenting the people of the Earth – those, who during the tribulations period, will choose to follow the Antichrist's policy and receive his diabolical mark on their foreheads or the back of their hands. Immediately following this judgement of God during the tribulation period, the Word of God, in Revelation, predicted that the sun will become completely darkened. The Bible says this darkness will be so great until the people of the Earth will gnaw on their tongues for pain. And yet, they will not repent of their evil deeds, but will look toward the heavens, blaspheming and cursing God the more. (Revelation 16:8-11) This increased heat of the sun, followed by complete darkness sounds like a nova to me. How does it sound to you?

Jesus Christ predicted, in the last days there shall be signs in the sun and I propose to you, Beloved, that these increased sunspots on our sun could very well be the signs He was speaking of.

He also predicted that there will be signs in the moon and stars. Do you realize that ever since the beginning of time, man has had the desire to go to the moon? For thousands of years, mankind has had this craving, but never had the tools and know how until our generation. In 1969, when the United States of America sent a spacecraft over 175,000 miles away, landing on the moon's surface, a man climbed out of the craft and walked on the moon! Since that miraculous moment in 1969, there have been many others who have set foot on the moon and walked.

Mankind has also sent spacecrafts to Mars, landing on its surface, sending data back to Earth about this distant planet. Man has sent spacecrafts far beyond Mars, exploring our solar system and planets, making known to us many mysteries of the stars, planets and moons of our universe. I propose to you that man's invention of these spacecrafts, flying around outer space and landing successfully on the moon, mankind's walking on the moon's surface, leaving flags along with other man-made devices, and man's launching of high-tech spacecrafts flying to Mars and beyond into the universe sending information back to Earth about the planets and stars could possibly be some of the signs in the moon and stars which Jesus predicted would take place just prior to His return.

Jesus also said, in Luke 21, there will be signs upon the Earth such as distress of nations with perplexities; the sea and waves roaring. Truly, we are living in that time. For there has never, in the history of mankind, been a time as today where there is such distress of nations because of the threats of wars. We are living in a time where a single day never goes by without a war of some kind or act of terrorism is taking place somewhere in the world. These wars and acts of terrorism have been causing great distress of nations in recent times.

Jesus also said there will be perplexities of nations. What does perplexity mean? Great fear, confusion, puzzled, "No way out." What a true picture of the thoughts in the minds of the nations in our generation. There are so many adverse and disturbing things taking place in our world. Years ago, it was the rise of the deadly AIDS virus, but more recently the deadly Coronavirus. Also, disturbance is coming from the breaking up of our earth's ozone layer, food and water famines, increased crimes in our cities (such as murder and rape), drugs (crack, cocaine, opioids), riots, racial prejudice, social injustice, mental health and poverty. These kinds of things, just to name a few, are causing great perplexities of nations and there seems to be "no way out" of these problems. These, according to Jesus Christ, are signs of His soon return.

Jesus predicted that the seas and waves will be roaring in the last days. It is a known fact that hurricanes and tidal wave activity have dramatically increased in the last 15 years. The great devastating hurricanes and tidal waves are destroying billions and billions of dollars in property in several nations and islands of the seas and have claimed thousands upon thousands of human lives in recent years!

Jesus also said, "men's heart will be failing them for fear and for looking after those things which are coming upon the Earth." We are living in a generation where the number one killer of man is heart disease. Over the past 4o years, the largest increase in deaths has been from this disease. And more and more people are dying of heart attacks than in any other time in history. Why? It's not all caused by cholesterol; One of the main reasons is the rapid increase of stress upon the hearts of men and women because of the dangerous conditions lurking about in our society. There is so much stress and perplexity until all one has to do is click on the news, read the top stories, and one could have a heart attack. Or one could watch the local or national news for half an hour and his heart could be negatively disturbed for there is so much trouble in our world.

Jesus Christ predicted further in Luke 21 that, *"The powers of heaven shall be shaken."* What did He mean there? He wasn't talking about the third and second heavens where God and the holy angels dwell, for they cannot be shaken. But He was talking about the atmospheric heaven, where the clouds and elements of the sky dwell. Jesus said this part of Heaven, the lowest Heaven, will be shaken. The word *shaken* comes from the Greek word *sal-yoo,* which means disrupted. This word, disrupted means out of order, disarranged, disarrayed and mixed up. Jesus Christ was predicting that just prior to His return, the atmospheric heavens: The weather conditions would be disrupted, mixed up and out of order. We truly have witnessed an increase in this kind of activity in recent years where the weather conditions have been mixed up and out of order. Many times, when it should be hot, it is cold; And when it should be cold, it is hot. For instance, one night on June 21, 1992 (the first day of summer), the temperature here in Detroit, Michigan, was in the thirties. My wife and I turned on the furnace and placed a couple of blankets on our bed. This is mixed up and out of order. The temperature should have been in the seventies or eighties this time of the year.

There has been an increase in abnormal weather conditions all over the world. In several locations of the Earth, we are experiencing unusual drought conditions, destroying crops in record numbers. It seems that the weather, lately, has gotten out of control. Jesus foretold us that this day would come just prior to His return.

Right after Jesus listed these signs, which we just mentioned, listen to the very next words that proceeded from His mouth. *"And then shall they see the son of man (Jesus) coming in a cloud with power and great glory."* Right after these signs take place, the Lord will return. Now look at the 28th verse, *"And when these things begin to come to pass, then look up, and lift up your heads for your redemption draweth nigh."* Notice, He didn't say these signs would take place over several decades, but He said when these things (signs) "begin" to come to pass. When these signs "begin" to happen in the world, then you look up, Church, and lift up your heads for your redemption "the rapture" draweth nigh. Can you see how close we are to the Lord's return? For every sign which Jesus gave of His return has truly begun to come to pass.

In the same 21st chapter of Luke, Jesus gave a parable of a fig tree.

> ...*Before the fig tree and all trees; When they now shoot forth (bud), ye see and know of your own selves that summer is now nigh at hand. So likewise ye, when ye see these things come to pass, know ye that the kingdom of God is nigh at hand. Verily I say unto you, This generation shall not pass away, till all be fulfilled.*
>
> St. Luke 21:29-33

Now in order to grasp the full essence of this important parable, we must understand that this fig tree is symbolic to the nation of Israel. Jesus said when the fig tree shoots forth (or begins to bud and blossom), one could know or discern that summertime is near. We know this is true with a natural tree. We know that when a natural fig tree or any tree begins to bud and blossom on its branches, that summer could not be far away. But how does this parable apply to the nation of Israel?

Jesus was speaking about the rebirth of the nation of Israel in 1948. In the year of 70 A.D., the great Roman army, under the leadership of Titus, marched into Jerusalem and destroyed the Holy City, slaughtering thousands of Jews and taking the entire city captive. Those who escaped death were led away captive into many different nations of the world. (St. Luke 21:20-24) And the nation of Israel was inhabited and governed by Gentiles for over 1800 years as a result of this invasion. **"And Jerusalem shall** be trodden down of the Gentiles until the times of the Gentiles be fulfilled." (St. Luke 21:24) This fulfillment of the Gentile's time of inhabiting and ruling Israel's land was 1948 when the United Nations voted to allow the Jewish people to reclaim their homeland and become a nation again. For hundreds and hundreds of years, the Jewish people were a people in the world without a home, scattered all over the globe; but the Spirit of God moved upon the hearts of the world to give them back their land. After this vote, there was a worldwide exodus of Jews, leaving foreign countries, returning to Palestine. They came by train. They came by boats and buses. They came by airplanes and cars. Some came by donkey and even by foot, but they came. And they came by the hundreds of thousands back to the blessed land which God had given them thousands of years ago. And as a result of this event, the prophecy of Ezekiel 37 was fulfilled. (Ezekiel 37:1-14) The wind of deliverance blew upon God's chosen ones in the four corners of the Earth. The sinews reformed within them, the flesh returned to their bodies and then God breathed His breath into their lungs "And they lived." They stood up upon their feet, an exceeding great army once again, which was desolate and parched for several centuries since the invasion of Titus in 70 A.D. *"When the poor and needy seek water, and there is none, and their tongue faileth for thirst, I the Lord will hear them, I the God of Israel will not forsake them. I will open rivers in high places, and fountains in the midst of the valleys: I will make the wilderness a pool of water, and the dry land springs of water. I will plant in the wilderness the cedar, the shittah tree, and the myrtle, and the oil tree, I will set in the desert the fig tree, and the pine, and the box tree together: That they (the nations of the world) may see and know, and consider, and understand together, that the hand of the Lord hath done this (restoration of the land of Israel) and the holy one of Israel hath created it."* (Isaiah 41:17-20)

Therefore, the vote for the statehood of Israel, the great Exodus of Jews returning to their beloved homeland, the miracle of the parched, desolate land of Israel suddenly becoming fruitful and beautiful in 1948, is the budding and blossoming of the fig tree that are mentioned in the parable of Luke 21.

Jesus said when the fig tree begins to bud and blossom, know that summer is near. In other words, He's saying when you witness the rebirth of Israel as a nation and their land, which was desolate, begin to flourish, then know that I am soon to return. Jesus said that this generation shall not pass until all be fulfilled. What generation was Christ speaking of? He was talking about the generation when the nation of Israel was rebirthed: 1948. Is it conceivable that the rapture could take place in our day? Could it be possible that we are this close to the second coming of Jesus Christ? This writer thinks so. According to the Scripture's predictions, I would be surprised if we went much further into the twenty first century before the Lord Jesus returns.

God warned us, *"Take heed to yourselves, lest at any time your hearts be over charged with surfeiting, and drunkenness, and cares of this life, and so that day come upon you unawares. For as a snare (to catch people unaware) shall it come on all them that dwell on the face of the whole Earth. Watch (stay awake, be alert, looking, and expecting something to happen) ye therefore, and pray always that ye may be accounted worthy to escape (make the rapture) all these things that shall come to pass, and to stand before the son of man."* (St. Luke 21:34-36) I am not trying to pinpoint it or say what day or hour the rapture will take place, but according to what we have studied thus far in this book, I believe it is safe to say we are in the midst of the season where the Lord will return. *"Maranatha! The Lord is coming soon."*

CHAPTER ELEVEN

RUSSIA IMAGINES AN EVIL THOUGHT

———— ꙮ ————

I want you to turn your attention to a significant prophecy which the prophet Ezekiel gave about 587 B.C. Back in the early nineteen nineties, I warned you, Beloved, don't be deceived and put into a state of spiritual slumber because of the recent events of peace in Russia and the Eastern European Bloc Nations. As I suggested, the peace agreement called Dayton and what seemed to be a change to good behavior by Russia will not last. For the day will come in the near future where Russia, along with several allies, will seek to carry out an abominable imagination that will shock the entire world. Truly the time is ripe for this diabolical imagination of theirs to be fulfilled. The Word of God is emphatic when it warns, *"For when they shall say peace and safety; then sudden destruction cometh upon them as travail upon a woman with child; and they shall not escape."* (I Thessalonians 5:3)

The Hebrew Prophet Ezekiel predicted under the anointing of the Holy Spirit that the day will come when a massive and powerful army along with many allies will march toward the land of Israel in an attempt to wipe the Jewish people clean off the globe. It is not perfectly clear when this event will take place. Some Bible theologians believe it will take place during the middle of the seven-year tribulation period. Some are convinced this great invasion will start right after the rapture. Others believe just before the rapture. I personally believe that the invasion could take place shortly before or within a year or two after the rapture.

Let's examine the prophecy, *"And the Word of the Lord came unto me (Ezekiel) saying son of man, set thy face against Gog the land of Magog, the chief prince of Meshech (a territory of the former Soviet Union) and Tubal (Turkey) and prophesy against him, and say, thus saith the Lord God; Behold I am against thee, O Gog, the chief prince of Meshech and Tubal: and I will turn thee back, and put hooks into thy jaws, and I will bring thee forth, and all thine army, horses and horse men, all of them clothed with all sorts of armor, even a great company with bucklers and shields, all of them handling swords (weapons) Persia, Ethiopia, and Libya with them; all of them with shield and helmet: Gomer and all his bands (troops); the house of Togarmah of the north quarters, and all of his bands (troops): And many people (many other allies) with thee."* (Ezekiel 38:1-6)

Those of us who study end time prophecy understand that the word Gog in the prophecy represents the leader of Russia at the time of the invasion. Bible scholars also understand that the word Magog represents the nation of Russia (the chief prince of Meshech and Tubal). If one would search out historical genealogies, they would find this to be accurate. Persia in this prophecy represents the modern-day nations of Iraq and Iran. Togarmah of the north quarters represents the modern-day nation of Turkey. Ethiopia in the prophecy, represents several northern African nations. Also, the nation of Libya is mentioned and also Gomer, which is a territory of the former Soviet Union. Their descendants over time, have disbursed and migrated throughout Eastern Europe. The prophecy states that these nations along with many others in that region, will be involved in this massive invasion of tiny Israel. Why?

One reason is that it has been a well-known fact that Russia and several other nations have for many decades hated the Jews and their nation. Also, many Bible scholars believe the abundant natural resources flourishing in the land is coveted by less fortunate countries such as Russia. The value of the abundant mineral deposits in the Dead Sea alone has been estimated at trillions of dollars. There is enough potash in that sea to provide the needs of the entire world for over eighteen hundred years. With the increased threat of famine in the world, this potash becomes an extremely valuable substance that can be used as fertilizer. The wealth of this potash in Israel's Dead Sea is worth more than the combined wealth of France, England and the United States. As famine for food in less fortunate countries (including Russia) increases in the last days, this potash in the Dead Sea will become more and more significant for food production. This may very well be the main reason for the invasion.

Yet another reason for the invasion could be that these northern nations are envious of Israel's incredible technology. Israel has rapidly become a world leader in technology and Russia, along with these other nations, has longed to possess this technology. The Jewish scientists are brilliant, and some nations would love to pick their brains and steal their technological ideas.

Because of God's blessings bestowed upon the prophet Abraham for his obedience, a long-long time ago, God promised that his seed, which would come on the scene afterward, would be greatly blessed. And as a result, their intelligence, skills and innovations in many areas of life have exceeded in the Earth. Many of the best scientists, doctors and innovators in the world are Jewish and several of them live in the land of Israel.

Russia and its allies will make a foolish choice in trying to curse the nation of Israel. They will ultimately find that one cannot curse those whom the Lord God has not cursed nor defy those whom He has not defied.

This mighty force of northern armies led by Russia will come down on the land of Israel like a massive dark thunderstorm cloud. The prophecy seems to indicate the invasion will catch the world off guard.

The prophecy says:

> *Sheba and Dedan, and the merchants of Tarshish, with all the young lions thereof, shall say unto thee (Gog), Art thou come to take a spoil? Hast thou gathered thy company (allies) to take a prey? to carry away silver and gold, to take away cattle and goods, to take a great spoil?*

Ezekiel 38:13

Sheba and Dedan represent nations like Saudi Arabia, Bahrain, Dubai and other Persian Gulf nations. Tarshish, during the time of the prophecy, would eventually become the modern-day United Kingdom, England. For a long time, the national symbol of England has been the lion. Who are the young lions of England? Her off springs: those who have come from her, including America, Canada, Australia, etc. All of these nations and others will protest the invasion. "Russia" are you coming down to take a spoil? To take a prey? To take away Israel's gold? What are you doing? The prophecy seems to indicate this invasion will be so well planned and conspired until all of the friends of Israel will be so caught off guard and surprised until it will be too late to stop the invasion.

As the invasion attempt gets closer and closer to Palestine, Israel's only hope will be that the God of Abraham, Isaac and Jacob will intervene as He did many times in the days of old, and He will.

The God of Israel continued to speak through Ezekiel, *"Be thou prepared, and prepare for thyself, thou (Russia) and all thy company (Russia's allies) that are assembled unto thee, and be thou a guard unto them... After many days thou shalt be visited: In the later years (last days) thou shalt come into the land (Israel) that is brought back from the sword, and is gathered out of many people, against the mountain (nation) of Israel, which have been always waste: But is brought forth out of the nations, and they shall dwell safely, all of them. Thou shalt ascend and come like a storm, thou and all thy bands, and many people (allies) with thee (Russia). Thus, saith the Lord God; it shall also come to pass, that at the same time shall things come into thy mind, and thou shalt "Think an evil thought: And thou shalt say, I will go up to the land of unwalled villages (Israel); I will go to them that are at rest, that dwell safely, all of them dwelling without walls, and having neither bars nor gates. To take a spoil, and to take a prey; to turn thine hand upon the desolate places that are now inhabited and upon the people (Israel) that are gathered out of nations, which have gotten cattle and goods (prosperity) that dwell in the midst of the land."* (Ezekiel 38:7-12)

In these verses, God is informing us that the Russian army and its allies will be well prepared for this invasion. The invasion will not be a spare-of-the-moment attack, but it will be a very well-organized and planned strategy by these nations. This massive invasion will perhaps have been secretly planned for several years. God said that this attack will take place in the latter days and I believe it will most likely be shortly before the rapture or shortly after the rapture at the beginning of the tribulation period. God tells us that this invasion will take place during a time where Israel will be in a state of safety and their defense is off guard. Their enemies will come down upon them, says the Lord to take a spoil of Israel who will at the time be in a state of peace. The invasion will seem to catch the world by surprise and the only thing they will be able to do is send out a protest while the invasion is in process. (Ezekiel 38:13)

> *Therefore, thou son of man, prophesy against Gog, and say, Thus saith the Lord God; Behold I am against thee, O Gog, the chief prince of Meshech and Tubal:*

Ezekiel 39:1

God is saying I am against you Russia, not only for this invasion but for all of the evil devices you have stood for through many-many decades: your evil communism, countless acts of human rights violations and many attempts to steal elections in sovereign countries. I am against thee, Russia. I am against thee, O Russia, for your illegal seizures of peaceful nations by military force. I am against thee for your acts of oppression and poisoning of innocent people.

My friend, please read Ezekiel 38:19-23 and Ezekiel 39:1-16 to see the full extent of God's anger and judgement toward Russia in the future, according to end time Biblical prophecy in the Word of God.

As this great throng of armies led by Russia begins to come down on Israel and while they are arrogantly and systematically marching closer and closer toward Palestine, suddenly something miraculous will take place. The God of Israel will supernaturally intervene. The same God who parted the Red Sea, the one who performed the great miracles in Egypt before Pharaoh, will come forth. The God who brought down the great walls of Jericho, the God who led the children of Israel out of 400 years of bondage, leading them to the promise land with a pillar of a cloud by day and a pillar of fire by night. The God whose very presence in Israel's camp caused the great mountains and hills to tremble, skipping like little rams and lambs, will stand up between the land of His people and the millions of invading soldiers.

> *And it shall come to pass at the same time when Gog*
> *shall come against the land of Israel, saith the Lord*
> *God, that my fury shall come up in my face. For in my*
> *jealousy and in the fire of my wrath have I spoken.*
>
> Ezekiel 38:18-19

The God of Israel will fight for them as He did in the days of Moses and Joshua. He will send a very strong earthquake under the feet of this great throng of troops. He will send the spirit of pestilence among them swiftly and He will rain a devastating overflowing of hailstones mixed with fire and brimstone. This fury of almighty God will totally destroy these armies. There will be dead Russian bodies from those Israeli outskirts all the way back to Moscow.

In the 39th chapter of Ezekiel, the prophecy states that after God destroys this invading army, the Israelites will come forth and find millions of dead bodies. They will find an unbelievable number of tanks and several other large and small weapons and devices of war materials spread all over the plains. The Scriptures tell us the Israelites will burn these war machines and tools with fire. It will take seven years to finish the burning of them. It will be so many! And it will take seven-month's time to bury the dead of these armies!

God said, *"Thus will I magnify myself, and sanctify myself; and I will be known in the eyes of many nations, and they shall know that I (the God of Israel) am the Lord."* (Ezekiel 38:23)

CHAPTER TWELVE

THE TRIBULATION PERIOD

———— ༓ ————

The Apostle Paul wrote under the inspiration of the Holy Spirit *"The mystery of iniquity (spirit of Antichrist) doth already work, only He (the Holy Spirit) who now letteth (restrain) will let (restrain) until He (the Holy Spirit) be taken out of the way."* I am proposing to you in this book that we are very close to the time when the church and the Holy Spirit will be raptured to Heaven. When that takes place, then it will kick off the most devastating period of time that this world has ever known: "The tribulation period". As I stated earlier in this study, the tribulation period will last seven years. The first three and a half years will be the least devastating years, but the last three and a half years will be so horrible until the whole human race will be on the brink of total destruction because of wars, the Antichrist's massive executions, and the 21 judgements of Revelation.

I want you to turn your attention to the Book of Revelation, the 13th chapter, where Apostle John gave some details about the rise of the Antichrist in the world after the rapture.

And I (John) stood upon the sand of the sea, and I saw a beast rise up out of the sea, having seven heads and ten horns, and upon his horns ten crowns, and upon his heads the name of blasphemy. And the beast which I saw was like unto a leopard, and his feet were as the feet of a bear, and his mouth as the mouth of a lion: And the dragon gave him his power, and his great authority. And I saw one of his heads as it were wounded to death; and his deadly wound was healed: And all the world wondered after the beast. And they (the whole world) worshipped the dragon which gave power unto the beast; And they worshipped the beast, saying, who is like unto the beast? Who is able to make war with him? And there was given unto him a mouth speaking great things and blasphemies; and power was given unto him to continue forty and two months. And he opened his mouth in blasphemy against God, to blaspheme his name, and his tabernacle and them that dwell in Heaven. And it was given unto him to make war with the saints and to overcome them: And power was given to him over all kindreds, and tongues, and nations. And all that dwell upon the Earth shall worship him, whose names are not written in the Book of Life of the Lamb

slain from the foundation of the world. If any man have
an ear, let him hear.

Revelation 13:1-9

In this vision, Apostle John saw the rise of the diabolical Antichrist. In the first verse, the word sea was symbolic to a great multitude of people and nations. John said, as I was standing in the midst of this multitude, this beast which is the Antichrist had seven heads and ten horns and upon his heads the names of blasphemy. The seven heads and ten horns (with ten crowns on them) will be symbolic to the seven continents of the world and ten rulers of those regions of the Earth who will unite with the Antichrist in his quest to rule the world, but he will be their leader.

You might ask why the Bible calls the Antichrist a beast in Revelation 13. It is because this evil man will have the characteristics of a wild animal, a wild beast. Actually, he will have the characteristics and personality of a combination of three beasts all wrapped up into one. In the second verse, John described his beastly characteristic by saying he will be like a leopard. He will have feet as the feet of a bear and his mouth will be as the mouth of a lion. Of course, this does not describe what the Antichrist will look like, but it describes his nature. What is the nature of a leopard? A leopard is a dangerous animal, perhaps the most dangerous animal in all of the jungle because a leopard does not kill its prey always for food. Many times, he is known to kill just for the thrill of killing, leaving its victim without eating it. A leopard is tricky. That's why his cage in most zoos has the tightest security. A leopard in the wild is also known for stalking his potential victim for several miles without the prey being aware of his constant presence and toying with its victim by playing hide-and-seek in the bush or on the treetops for miles before he gets bored, then swiftly pounces on his prey. The Antichrist will be like a leopard.

He will also be like a bear. What is the nature of a bear? A bear is one of the most powerful predators of the jungle. He can be extremely vicious when he gets angry. He can rip his victims apart and devour them with his great claws and strength. The Antichrist will have a personality like that.

John said he will have a mouth like a lion. What is the nature of a lion? The lion is called the king of the jungle. When a lion walks about in the jungle, animals everywhere on the ground and in the treetops take special notice and are on alert. They give him 100 percent attention. They watch every step he takes and every direction he moves. They know that he is the king of the jungle and he can destroy them or their little ones in an instant. A lion is very powerful, and he walks around like he knows it. He has a proud and regal kind of disposition. The Antichrist will be like that: He will be powerful in the world, be king of the world, and as the lion, demand the respect of the entire world. He will walk around proudly and when he opens his mouth, he will speak arrogantly, and his leadership will be that of royal and regal as a great lion. Picture the characteristics of a leopard, bear and lion all wrapped up in one and you can clearly see why the Word of God calls this demon "the beast."

One might ask or wonder where this antichrist is coming from. Where is his origin? Revelation 11:7 reveals his origin.

And when they shall have finished their testimony, the beast that ascendeth out of the bottomless pit shall make war against them, and shall overcome them, and kill them.

Revelation 11:7

This Scripture tells us this beast, the Antichrist, will enter the world from the bottomless pit of Hell. He is coming from there because he is the son of Satan. From this pit, his seed will enter the world, being placed into the womb of a human woman and will be birthed into the world as a baby. Eventually, this baby will grow up from a child into a full-grown man. Satan is a copycat. The Godhead sent the Word (Jesus Christ) into the world from Heaven for a great mission, sending Him as a seed to be planted into the womb of a human woman (Mary) who gave birth to Him. The Word (Jesus) who became flesh eventually grew up into a full-grown man, carrying out his ultimate mission for the redemption of mankind. Satan, the copycat, will do the same kind of process, but for the purpose of evil with his son, the Antichrist. He too will eventually grow up into a full-grown man, and all along the years of his growth, as many will see him, be acquainted, and at times be in his presence, no one will know who he is. No one will know the depths of his ultimate purpose until the time of his diabolical satanic mission begins, following the rapture of the church.

Can you imagine what it will be like to live in his neighborhood, go to his elementary, middle, or high school? Or perhaps play with him on the playgrounds, go on a date with him, or attend a movie with him? Can you imagine having these kinds of experiences with the literal son of Satan, the child, the teen, the young adult, the son of perdition, the chosen one from the pit of Hell who would one day possess all of the devil's powers? Is it possible that this birth has already taken place? Could he already be a little boy, or perhaps a teen, or a young adult in the world right now? This writer thinks it is possible. I know that might sound a bit chilling, but we see all of the signs of the times taking place in the present day in which we live (the lying spirits running rapidly through a bad president, local and federal legislators, conspiracy theories being told and embraced all across the lands, the embracing of falsehood, and evil deceptions by multitudes of people as never before). Those of us who understand the Holy Scriptures know and realize that these things and these signs point to the fact that the spirit of the Antichrist is here diligently working behind the scenes and preparing for his time to soon step on the world stage as predicted by the Hebrew prophets of old.

As we read further in Revelation, the 13th chapter and the 3rd verse, John said, *"I saw one of the heads of this beast wounded unto death but the wound was healed."* This wounded head will be the Antichrist. Something will happen to him, causing him to die. It is believed, and the Scriptures seems to back up the fact, that there will be a coup led by three of his under associate leaders and they will be responsible for his assassination. His death will be known and broadcasted all over the globe. There will be a great shock and much grief because of his sudden death by assassination. It will probably be more shock and grief felt than that of the former United States President, John F. Kennedy's, sudden assassination in 1963. However, miraculously, the Antichrist's dead body will be revived and brought back to life to the amazement of the world. The world would've already adored him for his great contributions to world peace and prosperity on the Earth since he arose to power. However, his sudden rise from death will cause the world to immortalize him even more so. Can you recall how the majority of the United States loved J.F.K.? Just imagine how much more the majority would have loved him if he had somehow revived from death by assassination on that tragic November day in 1963. Now picture one who will be loved three times more than J.F.K. being revived from the assassin's bullet. That will give you an indication of how the world will react to the Antichrist being revived from assassination. After he is revived from death, John wrote, *"All of the world will wonder after the beast."* All of the world will love and adore him as never before.

As a result, the world will begin to worship the dragon (Satan) which gave the Antichrist his power. Their cry will be, "Who is like unto the beast? Who is able to make war with him? (or try to destroy him and his policy)." John wrote that this Antichrist will speak blasphemy against God during his period of leadership. The Word of God shows us in the sixth and seventh verse that he will open his mouth with great blasphemy against God blaspheming His Holy name. He will also, according to John's revelation, speak against God's tabernacle and those (the saints who made the rapture) who are dwelling in Heaven. And in the seventh verse of John's revelation, God shows us that the Antichrist will war against the saints on Earth and kill many of them. You might ask, who will be these saints greatly persecuted by the Antichrist during the tribulation after the rapture? After the rapture, eventually, around the halfway point of the seven-year tribulation, one hundred and forty-four thousand Jewish men will receive a revelation of the true Messiah: Jesus Christ. And they, under the anointing of God, will go forth into the world preaching and teaching Jesus Christ and Him crucified with great power and authority. They will be led by the prophets Elijah and Enoch, who will return from Heaven to Earth. Through these great prophets and the one hundred forty-four thousand Jewish believers, multitudes of Jews and Gentiles will get saved in the midst of the tribulation period. These Jews, along with those who will be led to Christ through their ministry, will refuse to follow the Antichrist's evil policy and as a result, will pay a great price for being servants of God during that time. More on this later.

Now continuing in Revelation, the 13th chapter, John said he beheld another beast coming up out of the Earth and this beast had two horns like a lamb but spoke as a dragon (11th verse). The second beast who joins in league with the Antichrist and becomes his greatest promoter, will be the great false prophet who will rise to power during the tribulation period. This false prophet will also be sent by Satan to deceive the world. He will possess great powers, do great miracles, and wonders in the Earth, such as causing fire to come down from Heaven (the atmospheric Heaven, which is the visible sky). And through his abilities to do great miracles and wonders, he will convince the world that the Antichrist is God, deceiving them to follow him and the false prophet. He will be far eviler than any false prophet who ever lived. The false prophet will convince the people of the Earth to build a replica statue of the Antichrist and cause the statue to come to life and speak to the world, telling them to bow and worship him. The false prophet will proclaim that any who refuse to bow and worship the image of the Antichrist will be executed.

Remember when I spoke earlier about the Antichrist's assassination? It will be the false prophet who will be responsible for raising him from the dead before the whole world. Can you see how the nations of the world will be deceived by this Satanic trio (Satan, the Antichrist, and the false prophet)?

> *And he (the Antichrist) causeth all, both small and great, rich and poor, free and bond, to receive a mark in their right hand, or in their foreheads: And that no man might buy or sell, save he that had the mark, or the name of the beast (Antichrist) or the number of his name. Here is wisdom. Let him that hath understanding count the number of the beast: For it is the number of a man; and his number is six hundred three score and six (666).*

Revelation 13:16-18

The number 666 will be his sign and those who dare to refuse to receive this number on their hand or forehead will not be permitted to buy (including food) or sell anything. You won't be able to get hospital care for you or your children. You won't be able to buy clothes nor any other necessities of life. And because of this stern policy, the majority of people will feel they have no other choice but to receive the mark. This will be a terrible time, for many children will betray their parents and parents will betray their children. Many parents will refuse the mark and some children who receive the mark will turn in their parents. Some parents or relatives will turn in their kindred. To most people in the world, the logical thing to do will be to receive the mark and avoid the wrath of the Antichrist and his followers.

However, I would like to sternly warn those of you who are living in that day: <u>Please do not worship the Antichrist, bow to his image, or receive the mark!</u> The repercussions and consequences will be far more devastating to you and your family in receiving the mark than rejecting it. Just look at what will happen to those who choose to worship the Antichrist and receive his mark.

> *And the third angel followed them, saying with a loud voice, if any man worship the beast (Antichrist) and his image (statue) and receive his mark (666) in his forehead or in his hand, the same shall drink of the wine of the wrath of God, which is poured out without mixture into the cup of his indignation; and he (those who receive the mark) shall be tormented with fire and brimstone in the presence of the lamb: And the smoke of their torment ascendeth up for ever and ever: And they have no rest day nor night, who worship the beast (Antichrist) and his image (statue) and whosoever receiveth his mark (666) of his name.*

Revelation 14:9-11

Yes, there will be many left behind after the rapture because they didn't prepare themselves properly, similar to the five foolish virgins in Matthew 25. However, if you are left behind, don't kill yourself and don't give up, Beloved, for there can yet be a ray of hope for you if you don't bow to the Antichrist's policy and instead receive Jesus as your Lord. God will raise up one hundred and forty-four thousand Jews along with Elijah and Enoch, who will show the way. Look for them, Beloved. For they will defy the Antichrist and his false prophet. They will powerfully proclaim the Gospel of our Jesus Christ throughout the world. Look for them, Beloved, and follow them. Always remember they will proclaim that Jesus Christ is the Messiah, and they will follow and diligently live after His ways according to the Holy Bible. And they will refuse to receive the mark of the beast. By these characteristics, you will know them. When you find them, follow them. (Zechariah 8:23)

My friend, I am not trying to persuade you that you can miss the rapture, and everything will be alright. However, I am informing you that there will be a little ray of hope for you; but you will suffer beyond measure in order to grasp this hope. If you miss the rapture, whatever you do, do not receive the mark of the beast (666) nor follow his evil system. If you sincerely repent to God and accept Christ into your heart by faith and obey His word, and you are executed by the Antichrist, God will have mercy on you and receive you into His heavenly kingdom. There will be multitudes around the world who will do this during the tribulation and make it to Heaven. These will be that number which no man could number who came out of great tribulation (the tribulation period). These saints will not go through light afflictions as most Christians go through in our day, but they will have to endure "great tribulation." They will be tortured; suffer great hunger and thirst. They will be betrayed by family. They will not be able to buy or sell. If they are caught, the Antichrist and his followers will cut off their heads. These are they who came out of "the great tribulation" (the tribulation period). Read Daniel 11:32-35 for more reference of those who will be saved during the tribulation period and the sufferings they will endure.

As I forestated, many will be executed by having their heads cut off for receiving Jesus as their Lord and Savior and for refusing to follow the Antichrist's policy. (Revelation 20:4) However, their souls will be immediately received up into Heaven to abide with the church that was resurrected during the rapture. Oh, what a great reunion and fellowship that will be! Those saints who came out of the great tribulation through execution will have a request for Jesus when they see Him in Heaven. Apostle John recorded it in Revelation 6:9-11:

> And I saw under the alter the souls of them that were slain for the Word of God, and for the testimony which they held: And they cried with a loud voice, saying how long, O Lord, Holy and true dost though not judge and avenge our blood on them (the Antichrist and his followers) that dwell on the Earth? And white robes were given unto every one of them; and it was said unto them, that they (the saints slain during the tribulation period) should rest (in Heaven with the raptured saints) yet for

a little season (three and a half years) until their fellow servants also and their brethren, that should be killed (executed having their heads cut off) as they were should be fulfilled.

In the 7th chapter of Daniel, the Prophet Daniel also had a vision about the rise of the Antichrist during the tribulation period. In his vision, he too described this evil man as a beast. He mentioned, as John did, about the ten horns (ten world leaders) who will join him (Daniel 7:8 and 7:20). He also reveals that the Antichrist will kill three of the world leaders, plucking them up by their roots. Many scholars believe these slain leaders will have been responsible for the assassination attempt of the Antichrist (Daniel 7:7-8). Note that the little horn mentioned in verse 8 of Daniel 7 is the Antichrist.

According to Daniel's accounts, the Antichrist will be a great orator: (Daniel 7:11) and (Daniel 7:20). Eventually, he will have the seven remaining world leaders under him removed from power. Daniel also confirms Apostle John's vision that the Antichrist will persecute, wear out and kill many of the saints who will get saved after the rapture (Daniel 7:21 and Daniel 7:25). And Daniel reveals that this evil man will cause laws and times to be changed during the tribulation period (Daniel 7:25). However, his reign of terror will eventually be broken by the returning to Earth of the "Ancient of Days" (Jesus Christ), who will come from Heaven to set up His throne of righteousness and we, His holy people, will rule with Him (Daniel 7:9-10 and Daniel 7:26-27). Now, I mentioned earlier a little about one hundred and forty-four thousand Jews who will accept Jesus Christ as the Messiah during the tribulation period. They, along with Elijah and Enoch, will preach the Gospel to the world during those troubling times. Let us examine these spiritual warriors and the return of Elijah and Enoch a bit further.

The Ministry of The 144,000

And after these things I saw four angels standing on the four corners of the Earth, holding the four winds of the Earth, that the wind should not blow on the Earth, nor on the sea, nor on any tree. And I saw another angel ascending from the east, having the seal of the living God: And he cried with a loud voice to the four angels, to whom it was given to hurt the Earth and the sea, saying, hurt not the Earth, neither the sea, nor the trees, till we have sealed the servants of our God in their foreheads. And I heard the number of them which were sealed: And there were sealed an hundred and forty and four thousand of all the tribes of the children of Israel. Of the tribe of Judah were sealed twelve thousand. Of the tribe of Reuben were sealed twelve thousand. Of the tribe of Gad were sealed twelve thousand. Of the tribe of Aser were sealed twelve thousand. Of the tribe of Nepthalim were sealed twelve thousand. Of the tribe of

Manasses were sealed twelve thousand. Of the tribe of Simeon were sealed twelve thousand. Of the tribe of Levi were sealed twelve thousand. Of the tribe of Issachar were sealed twelve thousand. Of the tribe of Zabulon were sealed twelve thousand. Of the tribe of Joseph were sealed twelve thousand. Of the tribe of Benjamin were sealed twelve thousand.

Revelation 7:1-8

The angels of destruction during the Tribulation will be instructed to not harm these one hundred forty-four thousand Jews, for they will be sealed (saved, accepting Christ as Lord). As you read the remaining verses of Chapter 7, you will find that a great multitude will also be saved during the Tribulation who will have washed their robes and made their lives clean through the blood of the lamb. The angel asked John in the vision, **"What are these (the great multitude) which are arrayed in white robes? And whence (where did they) come from"**? John said, Sir, I don't know, but you know. Then the angel said, **"These are they which came out of great tribulation."** This great multitude will be the group of people who will refuse to receive the mark of the beast during the tribulation. They will choose rather to accept Jesus Christ as their Lord and Savior and as a result, they will go through the most horrible persecution any group of Christians has ever experienced in all of history. Their trials and persecution will far exceed the trials of us who will have made the rapture a few years earlier and these people will have to resist

Satan unto blood (Hebrews 12:3-4). They will know what it is to die for the Gospel of Jesus Christ. **"These are they which came out of great tribulation."**

It is believed by many end-time prophecy scholars that this multitude of people, who will be saved during the tribulation period, will be influenced by the ministry of the one hundred and forty-four thousand Jewish believers along with Elijah and Enoch. This chapter along with other passages also indicates this belief. The one hundred and forty-four thousand Jews will be all men. They will be virgins. And during those years, they will be powerful and pure vessels in God's hands, and this will be their testimony:

> *And they sung as it were a new song before the throne, and before the four beasts, and the elders: and no man could learn that song but the hundred and forty and four thousand, which were redeemed from the Earth. These are they which were not defiled by women; for they are virgins. These are they which follow the Lamb withersoever he goeth. These were redeemed from among men, being the first fruits unto God and to the Lamb. And in their mouth was found no guile: for they are without fault before the throne of God.*
>
> Revelation 14:3-5

fire proceedeth out of their mouth, and devoureth their enemies: And if any man will hurt them, he must in this manner be killed." These (Elijah and Enoch) have power to shut Heaven that it rain not in the days of their prophecy (3 ½ years, during the last half of the tribulation period): And have power over the waters to turn them to blood, and to smite the Earth with all plagues, as often as they will (desire). And when they shall have finished their testimony, the beast that ascendeth out of the bottomless pit shall make war against them, and shall overcome them, and kill them.

Revelation 11:3-7

God will give Elijah and Enoch power and authority to prophecy in the Earth for a thousand two hundred and seventy days (three and a half years). Revelation 11:4 says these are the two olive trees spoken of in Zechariah's prophecy (Zechariah 4:11-14) who would stand before the God of the Earth in the last days. The Word of God says in Revelation 11:5 that if any man tries to hurt them, God's fire will come forth out of their mouths and destroy them. Wow! They will be some powerful men.

The Word of God says in the 6th verse these prophets (Elijah and Enoch) will have the power to shut up Heaven that there be no rain. They will lift up their holy hands to Heaven and have the power to turn the rivers and seas into blood. They will also be able to lift up their hands and summon many plagues upon the Earth as often as they choose.

Their demonstration of miraculous power will be God's way of punishing the Antichrist and his followers. However, those who get saved and don't receive the mark of the beast won't be harmed by these judgements. These two men of God, along with the one hundred forty-four thousand male Jewish virgins will be a great thorn in the Antichrist's side. He will fear them and hate them with a great passion. The seventh verse tells us when the time of the two prophet's ministry is over, the Antichrist (who came to the Earth from the bottomless pit: Hell) will finally kill Elijah and Enoch.

As you read on further in this chapter, you will find that the world will rejoice over their death. It's not clear how they will be killed. Perhaps they will be executed by a guillotine because this will be the Antichrist's method of execution during the tribulation. At any rate, we do know that the Antichrist will have Elijah and Enoch killed openly in Jerusalem. The Bible tells us that the Antichrist will not allow the prophet's bodies to be buried for three days but will make an open shame of them by keeping their corpses on display in the streets of Jerusalem for all the world to see. The Bible tells us that all of the world will be able to look at their dead bodies and they (the Antichrist's followers) will rejoice over this sight, make merry and even exchange gifts. Their tormentors, the ones who sent great plagues upon them for three and a half years are finally dead. This display of the prophet's dead bodies most likely will be televised by the Antichrist by way of satellite or live stream to the four corners of the Earth, causing rejoicing, partying and much happiness all over the world to all of those who have the mark of the beast.

But in the midst of this great party, something miraculous will take place. The Bible tells us after three and a half days, the spirit of life from God will enter into the prophet's dead bodies and Elijah and Enoch will stand upon their feet for the Antichrist and all of the world to see. Can you imagine the impact of this, Beloved? These two great prophets, whose dead bodies will have been on display before the whole world in the streets of Jerusalem for over three days will suddenly stand up alive and well. People most likely will be running and screaming everywhere to the top of their lungs, including the Antichrist. For those who they feared for three and a half years will have suddenly come back to life.

After they come back to life and stand up upon their feet, the prophets will hear God's voice saying, **"Come up hither."** They will ascend up to Heaven in a cloud as their enemies in Jerusalem and over the world will watch in person and through live stream video.

The Bible says in that same hour after they are lifted to Heaven, God will send an earthquake and the tenth part of the city will

THE MYSTERY OF INIQUITY

be destroyed, killing seven-thousand of those who made a mockery of the death of these prophets. Those who escape the earthquake in that city will be greatly frightened and begin to give praise to the God of Elijah and Enoch.

The Twenty-One Judgements of Revelation

We are talking about the tribulation period, the most devastating span of time in the history of the human race. Please don't miss the rapture, Beloved, for you would not want to live on this Earth during that time. There will be twenty-one judgements that will fall upon the Earth during the tribulation period. These judgements will come as a result of those two great prophets lifting their hands toward Heaven against those in the world who will choose to defy their creator and worship the diabolical Antichrist. Apostle John saw every one of these twenty-one judgements in his vision while he was in the spirit on the Lord's day (the tribulation period). He saw seven seal judgements, seven trumpet judgements and seven bowl judgements. The following are the accounts of what he beheld in the vision.

The Four Horsemen of Revelation

In the sixth chapter of Revelation, John saw "a rider on a white horse with a crown on his head and a bow in his hand without an arrow" and the Bible says he shall go forth conquering and to conquer. The rider on the white horse will be symbolic of the rise of the Antichrist during the tribulation.

When the second seal was loosed in Revelation six, John saw "**a rider on a red horse with a sword.**" This was symbolic of the spirit of war striking many upon the Earth during the tribulation period. When the third seal was loosed, John saw "**a rider on a black horse with a pair of balances in his hand.**" This represented great famines, famines much more devastating than the world has ever known.

When the fourth seal was loosed, John saw "**a rider with a sword on a pale horse.**" This means death. Through this judgement, one-fourth of the world population will be destroyed. If we use the current population, nearly 2 billion will die because of this fourth seal judgement during the tribulation period.

The Remaining 17 Judgements of Revelation

When the fifth seal was loosed, John saw a multitude of people who had been murdered by the Antichrist because they refused to receive his mark.

When the sixth seal was loosed, John said:

> There was a great earthquake; and the sun became black as sackcloth of hair, and the moon became as blood; And the stars of heaven fell unto the Earth, even as a fig tree casteth her untimely figs, when she is shaken of a mighty

wind. And the heaven departed as a scroll when it is rolled together; and every mountain and island were moved out of their places. And the kings of the Earth, and the great men, and the rich men, and the chief captains, and the mighty men, and every bondman, and every free man, hid themselves in the dens and in the rocks of the mountains; And said to the mountains and rocks, fall on us, and hide us from the face of him that sitteth on the throne, and from the wrath of the Lamb (Jesus): For the great day of his wrath is come; and who shall be able to stand?

Revelation 6:12-17

When the seventh seal is loosed something very strange will happen. There will be complete silence in Heaven for the space of a half-hour. Why? It is believed that the 14 judgements that are to follow this seventh seal will be so awesome and devastating until even the celestial beings in glory will be moved to silence.

When the first trumpet is sounded by an angel in Revelation the eighth chapter, hail, fire and blood will fall upon the Earth, causing one-third of all trees and grass to burn. When the second trumpet is sounded, a falling meteor will destroy one-third of ships, one-third of fish and one-third of the sea will be filled with blood.

When the third trumpet sounds, more falling stars will poison one-third of all drinking water on the Earth. When the fourth trumpet sounds, one-third of the sun, moon and stars will become darkened. When the fifth trumpet sounds, the monstrous-looking locust that I mentioned earlier in the book will ascend from the bottomless pit to torment men for five months.

When the sixth trumpet is sounded, in Revelation the 9th chapter, four monstrous creatures will ascend out of the River Euphrates and destroy one-third of mankind. That's nearly 2 billion based on today's population count). In the eleventh chapter of Revelation, John saw the great earthquake which killed seven thousand of those who made merry of the death of Elijah and Enoch.

Then, John saw the seven-vial judgement. In the first vial judgement, John saw malignant sore boils break out on all people who had the mark of the beast. Also, in the 16th chapter of Revelation, when the second vial judgement was poured out on the Earth, John saw the entire sea become as blood of men and everything living in the sea died. When the wrath of the third vial judgement was poured out upon the Earth, John saw all of the rivers and springs turn into blood. When the fourth vial judgement was poured on the Earth, John saw the sun begin to get extremely hot, scorching those who had the Antichrist's mark.

When the fifth vial was poured, there was a great darkness that completely covered the Earth. When the sixth vial is poured out, the great River Euphrates will dry up and an army of some two hundred million from the far east will begin to march toward a historical valley called Armageddon. When the seventh and final vial shall be poured upon the Earth, an exceedingly great earthquake, such as was not seen since men were upon the Earth, will strike and also great hailstones will fall on the Earth, destroying all cities. Each one of these hailstones will weigh about one hundred pounds each! Do you want to miss the rapture and live in the world during this span of time? Meditate deeply about this significant question, my friend!

CHAPTER THIRTEEN

JACOB'S TROUBLE

———⟡———

A las! *"For that day is great, so that none is like it: It is even the time of Jacob's trouble: but he shall be saved out of it."* (Jeremiah 30:7) This was a prophecy in about 606 B.C., by Jeremiah about a great time of trouble that will come upon the Jewish people during the Tribulation period. The prophet cried, "**Alas!**" which means woe, great destruction. There will be none like this day. I am sad to write that this time of trouble for Israel will be amongst the worst in Jewish history. Jeremiah said, "**Alas!**" It is an event in the time of Jacob's (Israel's) trouble, but there will be a ray of hope. For God said, through the prophet, "**Israel shall be saved out of it.**"

Just exactly what is Jacob's trouble? What will be the cause and effect upon the Jewish people? Let's examine in this chapter. When Jesus Christ (the Messiah) was here on Earth two thousand years ago, He spoke some very profound words of prophecy to His beloved people, Israel. He said, "**I am come in** my father's name, and ye received me not: If another shall come in his own name, him ye will receive." (St. John 5:43) For thousands of years, the Jewish people have been looking and waiting for a great deliverer, a Messiah, who will be sent to the Earth by God to cause the threats of their enemies to cease, restore Israel to world power, and bring an everlasting peace on Earth. According to the Hebrew prophets, this Messiah would come with great power and majesty, dressed in regal apparel. He would come as a ruler and a conquering King to rule the Earth according to the Word of God.

Jesus Christ did not come in this royal apparel. He didn't come in great majesty, ruling the kingdoms of the world. He came meek and lowly. He came born in a little manger in the slums of Bethlehem. He had no great robe of regal. He had no beautiful and majestic crown on His head, and He did not restore Israel back to world power. Nor did He cause the threat of their enemies to cease. Therefore, for this cause, they rejected Him and refused to believe this man, Jesus Christ, could possibly be their Messiah, King of the Jews.

> *For I would not, Brethren, that ye should be ignorant of this mystery, lest ye should be wise in your own conceits; that (spiritual) blindness in part is happened to Israel, until the fullness of the Gentiles be come in.*
>
> Romans 11:25

Because of Israel's rejection of the Messiah, God opened the door to the Gentiles and brought the message of salvation and redemption to them.

> *"He (Jesus Christ) came unto his own (the Jews), and his own received him not. But as many as received him (the Gentiles), to them gave he power to become the sons of God, even to them that believe (He is the Messiah) on his name."*

St. John 1:11-12

What many of the Jews did not realize was that their Holy Scriptures clearly speak of the Messiah coming twice to the Earth before Armageddon. The first time as a savior, a sacrificial lamb with a meek and humble spirit to deliver all mankind from the bondage of sin. The Hebrew prophets clearly reveal that the Messiah would be afflicted and killed for an offering of righteousness to save man from a burning Hell as a result of Adam's disobedience in the Garden of Eden. Please study the following Old and New Testament Scriptures carefully: Psalms 69:19-21, Isaiah 50:6-7, Hebrew 7:24-27, Hebrews 4:15-16, Hebrews 10:1-5. These Scriptures explain how the Messiah would come the first time and why He came the way He did.

There is another prophecy in the Old Testament which many Jews somehow missed because of spiritual blindness. This prophecy clearly speaks of the Messiah coming as Jesus did that first time over two thousand years ago.

Who have believed our report? And to whom is the arm of the Lord revealed? For he (the Messiah) shall grow up before him (God the Father) as a tender plant, and as a root out of the dry ground: He (the Messiah) is despised and rejected of men; a man of sorrows, and acquainted with grief: And we hid as it were our faces from him; he was despised, and we esteemed him not. Surely he hath borne (carried) our griefs, and carried our sorrows: Yet we did esteem him stricken, smitten of God, and afflicted. But he was wounded for our transgressions, he was bruised for our iniquities: The chastisement of our peace was upon him; and with his stripes we are healed. All we like sheep have gone astray; we have turned everyone to his own way; and the Lord hath laid on him (the sacrificial lamb) the iniquity of us all. He was oppressed, and he was afflicted, yet he opened not his mouth: he is brought as a lamb to the slaughter, and as a sheep before her shearers is dumb, so he (the Messiah) openeth not his mouth. He was taken from prison and from judgement: and who shall declare his generation? For he was cut off out of the land of the living: For the transgression of my people was he stricken. And he made his grave with the wicked, and with the rich in his death; because he had no violence, neither was any deceit in his mouth.

Isaiah 53:1-9

My beloved Jewish brothers and sisters, the great prophet Isaiah was clearly speaking under the inspiration of God concerning your Messiah's first of three comings. He died a sacrificial lamb over two thousand years ago on Mount Moriah for our sins. But three days later, He arose from the grave with all power, dominion and authority. He is in Heaven, my beloved Jewish brothers and sisters, right now sitting on the right hand of Jehovah God, making intercession for those who call upon His name. (Joel 2:32 and Acts 4:10-12) Truly, **"the stone which the builders rejected has become the head of the corner."** (St. Luke 20:17)

The Messiah had three great missions. The first was completed over two thousand years ago when He came meek and lowly as a sacrificial lamb to be crucified and die for our sins. The Messiah's second mission which is to return in the clouds of glory and rapture the dead in Christ and also those who are alive and remain during the rapture which is soon to take place. The Messiah's third mission will be to once more return during the battle of Armageddon and restore Israel to world power, making the land of Israel the capital of the world. His stopping the threat of Israel's enemies and bringing world peace and harmony has not happened as of yet. Many Jews don't realize and will be shocked to find out when this Messiah returns the third time, He will be the one they have rejected and despised for over 2,000 years. Jesus Christ told the Jews, **"I am come in my father's name, and ye received me not: If another shall come in his own** name, him ye will receive." (St. John 5:43) This one who will come in his own name to the Jews will be none other than the diabolical Antichrist. And just as Jesus Christ predicted, many Jews will receive this false messiah, the son of Satan, who will ascend from Hell. And this great mistake by Israel will be the beginning of Jacob's trouble.

How will this possibly happen? It is believed, the crisis in the Middle East region will continue to escalate until, eventually, it threatens the peace of the whole world. The world will be on pins and needles as never before because of the constant possibility of world war as a result of the escalation of controversy between Jews and Arabs.

In the midst of this great growing problem will arise a man, a great negotiator, who will have already gained somewhat growing influence and popularity in the world. This man somehow, someway, will accomplish something scores of leaders of years past could not accomplish. He will bring peace to the Middle East and solve the great controversy. This noble accomplishment will captivate the entire world and will be one of the catalysts of his elevation to world rulership. He will be called a brilliant statesman for his great accomplishment, along with his many other brilliant achievements in the world. The world will begin to worship him and his greatness. They will cry, "Who is like unto this man." (Revelation 13:4)

He will also win the hearts of the Jews in Israel, for he will begin to show acts of favor and kindness to them. He will make a strong covenant with them and guarantee their safety from their enemies. He will permit the Israelis to build a new temple on the site of Solomon's temple. Israel will be permitted to reinstitute the sacrifice and offerings as in the law of Moses. The permission to build a new temple for the first time in thousands of years right on the location of Solomon's temple and the rise of this royal and brilliant leader showing protection, favors and kindness to the Jews in Israel will convince many of the Israelis that this man is their Messiah who they had been waiting on for thousands of years. I can still hear the profound prophetic words of Jesus Christ in St. John 5:43, **"I am come in my Father's name, and ye receive me not: if another shall come in his own name, him ye will receive."** And yes, the Jews will receive this false messiah, the Antichrist, who will come in his own name. He will deceive the Jews by coming to their rescue as a wolf in sheep's clothing. He will make a covenant of peace with Israel.

Let's examine this. In Daniel 9:27 it reads:

> *And he (the Antichrist) shall confirm the covenant with many for one week: and in the midst of the week he shall cause the sacrifice and the oblation to cease, and for the overspreading of abominations he shall make it desolate, even until the consummation, and that determined shall be poured upon the desolate.*

This prophecy by Daniel describes just how the Antichrist will win the Jew's hearts. He will give them a "strong covenant," a seven-year pact (One week in this verse means seven years). He will give Israel some kind of seven-year pact protecting them and allowing them to reinstitute the Old Testament worship in the brand-new temple, which he will allow them to build on the sight of the temple destroyed by Titus in 70 A.D. This seven-year pact, this covenant will overwhelm the Jews in happiness, and they will begin to do their offerings, sacrifices and other forms of worship once again in a new temple for the first time in thousands of years. But in the midst of that seven-year pact, the wolf will suddenly remove his fake sheep clothes and reveal his true sinister character. He will walk into the temple in Israel, cause their offering and sacrifices to cease and demand they all bow down and worship him as God. Daniel says he will overspread abominations in that temple, breaking his false covenant and this will be the start of Jacob's trouble.

When the Israelis believe that this man is the Messiah and make this covenant or pact with him, they will not realize that they will be making "**A covenant with death**." The Prophet Isaiah saw this day coming and he prophesied about it.

Wherefore hear the Word of the Lord, ye scornful men (Jewish leaders who scorned the true Messiah), that rule this people which is in Jerusalem. Because ye have said, We have made a covenant with death, and with Hell are we at agreement; when the overflowing scourge shall pass through, it shall not come unto us: for we have made lies our refuge, and under falsehood have we hid ourselves... And your covenant (seven year peace pact) with death shall be disannulled (broken), and your agreement with Hell (Satan and the Antichrist) shall not stand; when the overflowing scourge (great persecution, Jacob's trouble) shall pass through, then ye shall be trodden down by it.

Isaiah 28:14-15, 18

I think this prophecy explains itself clearly. The covenant, which Israel's leaders (political and religious) will make with the Antichrist, will greatly anger their God. Their covenant of peace with the man of sin will turn into a covenant with death and Hell.

One day, perhaps on a Sabbath day, while the Israelis are in great attendance in and around the new temple, approximately three and a half years after they will have made a seven-year covenant with this man who they will choose to be their messiah. The Antichrist, along with the false prophet and many of his followers, will be in Jerusalem gathered there with many thousands and thousands of Jews in and around the temple. The Antichrist will sit on a throne within the temple, along with Jewish political and religious leaders. It is not fully clear what will be the occasion of this great gathering of leaders at the temple. Perhaps it will be to dedicate the finishing of the building process, but the Antichrist will be sitting on a throne in the midst of a throng of Jews.

The Antichrist will have a large, completely veiled object brought into the temple. The Jews will most likely believe that this object will be a present for the temple and the Jewish people in the dedication of the building. Tens of thousands of Jewish people will be there and witness the unveiling of the gift from their beloved messiah.

It will be during this seemingly harmless occasion and setting when the covenant of peace will turn into a covenant of death. For suddenly, the Antichrist's men will unveil this mysterious gift and underneath will stand a statue: A diabolical image of the Antichrist. The Jewish religious leaders will be shocked, for under the law of Moses, they were taught not to have a graven image in their temple. The false prophet will walk up to this statue and speak to it, causing it to come to life before everyone's eyes. (Revelation 13:15) This statue of the Antichrist will suddenly begin to talk to the Jewish leaders and people, demanding they bow and worship the Antichrist and his graven image, fulfilling Daniel's prophecy of the abomination of desolate (the image of the beast) being set up in the temple in the last days. (Daniel 12:11)

It will be at this uncomfortable and shocking moment that the Israelis will know that they made a great mistake. For they will know that according to the Holy Scriptures, their true Messiah would not demand that they bow and worship a graven image. They will know that this could not be the one they had been looking for.

This shocking and uncomfortable occasion will also fulfill the prophecy of Apostle Paul in II Thessalonians 2:3-5: **"And that man of sin (Antichrist) be revealed, the son of perdition: Who opposeth and exalteth himself above all that is called God, or that is worshipped; so that he as God, sitteth in the temple of God, shewing himself that he is God. Remember ye not, that, when I was yet with you I told you."**

Because of their strong commitment to the law of Moses, these Jewish religious leaders and thousands upon thousands of lay people will refuse to bow to the talking image of the beast. Nor will they bow or worship the Antichrist sitting on that throne in their temple demanding praise and obedience from all of Israel. Because of the Israeli's defiance, the rage of the Antichrist's evil spirit will wax hot and he will order the death and destruction of them all.

Over two thousand and five hundred years earlier, the Hebrew prophet, Jeremiah, cried out, **"Alas! (Woe, great destruction) For that day is great, so that none is like it: It is even the time of Jacob's (Israel's) trouble."** (Jeremiah 37:7)

Jesus warned the Jews and had it recorded in the Word of God. He told them,

> *When you therefore shall see the abomination of desolation (the image of the beast), spoken of by Daniel the prophet (Daniel 12:11, Daniel 9:27), stand in the holy place (the new temple built in Jerusalem during the tribulation period), (whoso readeth, let him understand): Then let them (the Jews) which be in Judaea flee into the mountains: Let him which is on the housetop not come down to take any thing out of his house: Neither let him which is in the field return back to take his clothes. And woe unto them that are with child, and to them that give suck in those days! But pray ye that your flight (escape, retreat) be not in the winter, neither on the sabbath day: For then shall be great tribulation, such as was not since the beginning of the world to this time, no, nor ever shall be. And except those days should be shortened, there should no flesh be saved: but for the elect's sake those days (the tribulation period) shall be shortened.*
>
> **St. Matthew 24:15-22**

Christ is describing here the unveiling of the image of the beast, mentioned in Daniel 12:11 and 9:27 and the aftermath. Jesus knew that the Jews would not bow to this image and He also knew the repercussions. So, He is warning the Jews here of the repercussions and tells them what to do. He is telling them when you see the abomination of the desolation which was prophesied by Daniel standing in the Holy temple, then understand and listen to my instructions. Run! Run my people, my chosen people! Run to the mountains of Israel for refuge. Don't try to go back to your houses or property to get your belongings or even your clothes, for you won't have the time.

Jesus said, woe unto the Jewish women who are pregnant on that day for they will be physically handicapped and won't be able to flee swiftly as others. And woe to their newborn babies, for they won't be able to defend themselves.

Jesus told the Jews to pray that this beginning of great tribulation for them doesn't happen in the wintertime nor on Sabbath day. Why did He say this? Because if this great persecution begins in the winter, many people will die from the elements in the mountains because they won't have time to get their warm clothes and blankets as they flee. And if it happens on the Sabbath day, many of the devout Jews will be slaughtered because they will refuse to use their cars, buses, trains, airplanes, or even donkeys to escape. As a result, they will be slaughtered by an unmerciful adversary. Christ went on to say this period of time will be a great tribulation, more devastating than any other time since the beginning of creation. Jacob's trouble will be worse than the Jews' experiences during World War II. It will be at this time where the immortal words of Jesus Christ (the

Messiah) spoken over two thousand years ago will have reached its fullest impact: "**Oh Jerusalem, Jerusalem, thou that killest the prophets, and stonest them which are sent unto thee, how often would I (the Messiah) have gathered thy children together, even as a hen gathereth her chickens under her wings, and ye would not!**" (St. Matthew 23:37)

Just how horrible will this day be? The prophet Zechariah summed it up in his prophecy over twenty-five hundred years ago.

> *And it shall come to pass, that in all the land, saith the LORD, two parts therein shall be cut off and die; but the third part shall be left therein. And I will bring the third part through the fire, and will refine them as silver is refined, and will try them as gold is tried: they shall call on my name, and I will hear them: I will say, it is my people: and they shall say, The Lord is my God.*
>
> **Zechariah 13:8-9**

This horrible Holocaust, this horrible tribulation and destruction of "two-thirds" of all Jews in Israel will be the result of their constant refusal to accept Jesus Christ as their Messiah for centuries. They will, however, accept the devil's son as their messiah and make a covenant with him. This will anger God in Heaven and He will step back for a season and allow their adversary to chasten them with heavy persecution. Zechariah said two-thirds of the Jews living in Israel on that day will be killed.

But God also revealed, through Zechariah's prophecy, that one-third will somehow survive this persecution and will eventually find their true Messiah. They will call upon Him and He will answer; they will call Him, their Lord, and He will call them, His people. This one-third, perhaps a few million Jews, will be those spoken of in the Book of Revelation and also in Zechariah, the 14th chapter:

> *And the woman (Israel) fled into wilderness, where she hath a place (ancient Petra) prepared of God, that they (angels?) should feed her (the Jews) there a thousand two hundred and threescore days (three and a half years).*
>
> Revelation 12:6

> *And to the woman (Israel) were given two wings of a great eagle, that she might fly (escape) into the wilderness, into her place (Petra), where she is nourished (by angels?) for a time (singular-one year), and times (plural-two years), and half a times (one half year) ... (for a total of three and a half years)*
>
> Revelation 12:14

> *...And thy spoil shall be divided in the midst of thee. For I will gather all nations against Jerusalem to battle; and the city shall be taken, and the houses rifled, and the*

women ravished; and half of the city shall go forth into captivity, and the residue (the remnant) of the people shall not be cut off from the city. Then shall the Lord (the true Messiah of Israel) go forth, and fight against those nations, as when he fought in the day of battle. And his feet (the Messiah's feet) shall stand in that day upon the mount of Olives, which is before Jerusalem on the east, and the mount of Olives shall cleave in the midst thereof toward the east and toward the west and there shall be a very great valley; and half of the mountain shall remove toward the north, and half of it toward the south. And ye (some of the one third of Jews who will escape the Antichrist) shall flee to the valley of the mountains; for the valley of the mountains (Moriah, Zion, Olives) shall reach unto Azal: yeah, ye shall flee, like as ye fled from before the earthquake in the days of Uzziah king of Judah: and the Lord (Messiah) my God shall come, and all the saints with thee.

Zechariah 14:1-5

The Legend of Ancient Petra

About one hundred miles south of Jerusalem lies an enchanting and mysterious rock fortress in the wilderness of Jordan called Petra. It has been called by many "The Red Rose City – half as old as time." Ancient Petra, which means "Rock," is a fortress city completely surrounded by great mountains. Inside of the surrounding mountains are a thousand large temples that were carved and artistically crafted out of the mountains. Some of you who watched Indiana Jones *The Last Crusade* saw a glimpse of one of those thousand temples near the end of the motion picture. They filmed the last part of the movie on location at ancient Petra in the late 1980s. Petra is so fascinating and mysterious it was recently voted by over one hundred million people as one of the seven wonders of the world. It has become the most visited tourist attraction in Jordan and one of the most visited archeological sites in the world.

Legend tells us that those who lived there in ancient times lived in a place that was considered to be impregnable and unconquerable. It has been said that the inhabitants of Petra could hold off great armies for months and even years with little rocks, bows and arrows and spears while standing on the tops of the clefts of the rocks. There was only one entrance for visitors to enter the great rock fortress and that was through a very narrow mile and a half long gorge. The inhabitants would pick apart the invading armies as the armies would have no choice but enter the city through this narrow, tedious pathway by foot or by horse in a single file.

The Edomites (Edom) were the first to live in the region of Petra about 1200 B.C. Around nine hundred years later, the Nabateans arrived and lived there for about four hundred years, beginning around three hundred and twelve B.C. One of the great mysteries of Petra is no one knows with one hundred percent certainty who built these amazing thousand temples surrounded by great mountains carved and crafted out of those mountains. Some have said it was the Nabateans. But, if it were them in those primitively ancient times, how in the world were they able to do such an awesome thing using ancient technology and instruments?

Personally, I believe these amazing temples were built by the Lord God's angels a long-long time ago before the Edomites and Nabateans arrived in preparation for the time of Jacob's trouble during the tribulation period, creating a place near Jerusalem for the Jews to escape of the Antichrist. Recall our Scripture text in Revelation 12:6: This place in the wilderness was prepared by God.

Many end-time prophecy theologians have been so convinced that many of the escaping Jews will flee to Petra that they have hidden thousands of New Testament Bibles in several locations within ancient Petra. These theologians are also convinced that many of these Jews surviving the Antichrist will wait in Petra being divinely protected until the Messiah comes.

Zechariah reveals that the other escaping Jews, who will flee to the mountains of Israel, will eventually hide in the valleys of mountains and be protected until the Messiah comes. It is in these places: Petra, the mountains of Israel and their valleys, where the remnant of Jews will flee and wait and pray for their true deliverer to come and save them. They will be divinely protected as they wait and be nourished for three and a half years. Once again, a terrible dictator will seek to totally wipe out the existence of the Jewish race. But he, like his predecessors, will not succeed. For God will shield and protect this remnant. He will not allow His chosen people to be totally destroyed. He promised in His Holy word:

> *Thus saith the Lord, which giveth the sun for a light by day, and the ordinances of the moon and of the stars for a light by night, which divideth when the waves thereof roar; The Lord of hosts is his name: If those ordinances (my laws) depart (cease) from before me, saith the Lord, then the seed of Israel also shall cease from being a nation before me for ever. Thus saith the Lord; If heaven above can be measured (by man), and the foundations of the Earth searched out beneath, I will also cast off all the seed of Israel for all that they have done, saith the Lord.*

Jeremiah 31:35-37

I think this Scripture explains itself. Israel will never be totally destroyed, and God's chosen people will always exist in the Earth. For the Almighty hath declared it!

CHAPTER FOURTEEN

THE BATTLE OF ARMAGEDDON

———— ೨ ೧ ೬ ————

There lies an enormously huge valley surrounded by mountains called Megiddo in the land of Israel. It is approximately thirty-five miles long and thirty miles wide. This historic region is called by some the valley of Jehoshaphat, and others have called it the plains or valley of Jezreel. However, it is better known by most as Armageddon. It is in this setting where the greatest war of all time will take place.

Many decisive battles have been fought in these plains in times past. It was in this place where the patriarch Barak defeated the Canaanites in 1316 B.C. (Judges 4:15) It was here where Gideon defeated the Midianites in 1256 B.C. (Judges 6:33) It was here where Josiah was killed in a war with Pharaoh Nechoh's Egyptian army in 624 B.C. (II Kings 23:29) And it was here where Saul and Johnathan died in battle against the Philistines. (I Samuel 31:1, II Samuel 1:16, 21)

Legend tells us that Napoleon Bonaparte once stood upon the surrounding mountains of Megiddo as he viewed this great valley and proclaimed, "All the armies of the world could maneuver for battle here." Indeed, he was correct. For one day, all of the armies of the world will maneuver in this valley, causing a horrible blood bath.

The question is, how will this great war in Armageddon begin? The Word of God does not give us complete details of what will trigger this war. However, the Bible does seem to indicate the kings of the Asian nations will eventually choose to rebel against the Antichrist's world rulership and assemble a great army to attack him and his troops in the land of Israel.

> *And the sixth poured out his vial upon the great river Euphrates; and the water thereof was dried up, that the way of the kings of the east might be prepared. And I saw three unclean spirits like frogs come out of the mouth of the dragon (Satan), and out of the mouth of the beast, and out of the mouth of the false prophet. For they are spirits of devils, working miracles, which go forth unto the kings of the Earth and of the whole world, to gather them to the battle of that great day of God Almighty. And he gathered them together into a place called in the Hebrew tongue Armageddon.*
>
> **Revelation 16:12-14 & 16**

Now the word *east* in the twelfth verse comes from the Greek word *anatoles heliou,* which means "the rising of the sun." This was the ancient designation of the oriental races. I am convinced that this army, which will rebel against the Antichrist, will be red China and perhaps a few other oriental nations. According to Revelation 9:16, this oriental army will be two hundred million strong! And it is a well-documented fact that Red China has been able (for many years now) to field an army of 200 million.

The Bible also tells us in the twelfth verse of Revelation 16 that somehow the great River Euphrates will dry up to prepare the way for these kings of the east and their multitudes. The drying up of the river will make the journey toward the land of Israel easier for horses, tanks, trucks and foot soldiers. This is when mighty China, who will have been vastly building up their industrialization and military might with much arrogance for many decades, will meet their ultimate fate and pay a heavy price for their evil deeds and diabolical ambitions as they march toward the middle east and eventually reach their destination of Armageddon. They will be emphatically broken by the King of kings and the Lord of lords, Jesus Christ. The Antichrist and his armies of the world will also prepare themselves for this rebellion and great invasion. He will assemble his legions from the whole Earth (according to Revelation 16) into this place called Armageddon. And so once again, the winds of war will blow and circulate from the four corners of the Earth, stirring troops to engage in a mighty battle.

The Scriptures do not tell us how many soldiers the Antichrist will assemble to confront the Asian armies, but it is safe to say he will at least have the same amounts of soldiers as his adversary. So, it is possible that there will be as many as four hundred million soldiers in this great conflict. Thus, this will be the most devastating battle in human history.

About twenty-seven centuries ago, the Prophet Joel saw this massive assembly of armies gathered to battle in a vision:

> ...*Prepare war, wake up (stir up) the mighty men, let all the men of war draw, near; let them come up. Beat your plowshares into swords, and your pruning hooks into spears: let the weak say, I am strong, assemble yourselves, and come, all ye heathen, and gather yourselves together round about: thither cause thy mighty ones to come down, O Lord. Let the heathen be wakened, and come up to the valley of Jehoshaphat (Armageddon): for there will I sit to judge all the heathen round about. Put ye in the sickle, for the harvest is ripe: come, get you down; for the press (valley) is full, the fats overflow; for their wickedness is great. Multitudes (hundreds of millions), multitudes in the valley (Armageddon) of decision.*

Joel 3:9-14

Meanwhile, in the spirit realm of the third Heaven, two more massive armies will be assembled, prepared to ascend to the

Earth for this great date with destiny. One of these two great armies assembled in Heaven will be none other than the Church, which was raptured from the Earth seven years earlier. The commander in chief of these two great merging armies will be the Messiah: Jesus Christ. Almighty God will assemble this army in Heaven in order to save the Jews who will be hiding in Israel and to save the world from being totally destroyed by this great war raging in the valley. The Bible says the war in Armageddon will be so devastating until the blood of men will come up to the horse's bridle. As the two massive armies are engaging in intense warfare, suddenly all of the focus will be changed toward the Palestinian sky. For in the midst of the war, something amazing will happen to cause all of the soldiers from both sides to look up toward the heavens. Apostle John described it this way:

And I saw heaven opened, and behold a white horse; and he that sat upon him was called Faithful and True, and in righteousness he doth judge and make war. His eyes were as a flame of fire, and on his head were many crowns; and he had a name written, that no man knew, but he himself. And he was clothed with a vesture dipped in blood: and his name is called The Word of God (Jesus Christ). And the armies (the angels and the raptured saints) which were in heaven followed him upon white horses, clothed in fine linen, white and clean. And out of his (Jesus) mouth goeth a sharp sword, that with it he should smite the nations (the evil armies gathered in

Armageddon): and he shall rule them with a rod of iron: and he treadeth the winepress of the fierceness and wrath of Almighty God. And he hath on his vesture and on his thigh a name written, KING OF KINGS, AND LORD OF LORDS... And I saw the beast (Antichrist), and the kings of the Earth, and their armies, gathered together to make war against him (Jesus) that sat on the horse, and against his army (the angels and us). And the beast was taken, and with him the false prophet that wrought miracles before him, with which he deceived them that had received the mark of the beast, and them that worshipped his image. These both were cast alive into a lake of fire burning with brimstone. And the remnant were slain with the sword of him that sat upon the horse, which sword proceeded out of his mouth (his spoken word): and all the fowls were filled with their flesh.

Revelation 19:11-16 & 19:19-21

This Scripture seems to indicate that once Jesus (and His armies in Heaven) cracks the sky above while the evil armies are engaging in warfare in Armageddon, they will stop fighting each other and turn their weapons toward the sky to fight our Lord, the angels, and the raptured saints as we descend upon white horses. Wow! This will be something! The Prophet David gives weight to this statement in his prophecy of Armageddon:

Why do the heathen rage, and the people imagine a vain thing? The kings of the Earth set themselves, and the rulers take counsel together, against the Lord, and against his anointed, saying, Let us break their bands asunder, and cast away their cords from us. He that sitteth in the heavens shall laugh: the Lord shall have them in derision. Then shall he speak unto them in his wrath, and vex them in his sore displeasure.

Psalms 2:1-5

The Antichrist and the armies in Armageddon will imagine "**a vain thought**" as the heavens are opened and the armies of Heaven come down. They will decide to try to fight God with their weapons. This will be extremely foolish. This is the reason why David cried; why? Why? Are these heathens thinking such a vain and foolish thought to fight God and His great heavenly hosts? It would be a wise choice for them to lay down their arms and surrender to God. But they will not. They will choose to defy the Lord to their death.

The Prophet Isaiah also saw this mighty event and prophesied about it:

Who is this that cometh from Edom, with dyed garments from Bozrah? This that is glorious in his apparel, travelling in the greatness of his strength? I that speak in righteousness, mighty to save. Wherefore art thou red in thine apparel, and thy garments like him that treadeth

173

in the winefat? I have trodden the winepress alone; and of the people there was none with me: for I will tread them in mine anger, and trample them in my fury; and their blood shall be sprinkled upon my garments, and I will stain all my raiment. For the day of vengeance is in mine heart, and the year of my redeemed is come.

Isaiah 63:1-4

In the vision, Isaiah asked the Lord, why is your garment red like someone that has been treading the wine fat? God's answer is this red stain all over His garment will be the blood of those who defy Him in this great battle. He told Isaiah He will trample them in great rage and fury. There are other Scriptures that clearly show that we, the raptured saints, will be right there with Jesus. I don't believe we will have to fight, but we will be there with Him. (Read Jude 1:14-15, St. Matthew 24:30-31 and Zechariah 14:3-5)

Some Bible scholars believe that immediately following the battle, Jesus and the saints will go to Petra and the mountains of Petra to console the remnant of Jews. If this is true, then this would explain why Isaiah cried, "**who is this that cometh from Edom?**" Petra is located in Edom. However, whether we see those Jews before or after the battle, I can assure you that we will meet them in Petra and the mountains and valleys of Israel. What a great event this will be! We, the raptured saints, will be able to tell those Jews what Heaven looks like, for we will have been there for seven years. What a joy that will be! We will hug, comfort and console those Jews with glad tidings. However, in the midst of this excitement, there will be sadness amongst the Jews. The Prophet Zechariah described it this way:

> *...and they shall look upon me whom they have pierced, and they shall mourn for him, as one mourneth for his only son and shall be in bitterness for him, as one that is in bitterness for his firstborn. In that day shall there be a great mourning in Jerusalem, as the mourning of Hadadrimmon in the valley of Megiddon. And the land shall mourn.... All the families that remain, every family apart, and their wives apart.*

> **Zechariah 12:10-12**

When these remaining Jews see Jesus in His royal apparel with all the power of a king in Heaven and the angels standing with Him; as they behold His hands and feet with the nail prints along with His pierced sides, they will finally realize that the one they have rejected for centuries is their Messiah. This realization will cause much grief in all of Israel. But the loving and compassionate Jesus will comfort His chosen people and wipe away their tears of sorrow.

The Antichrist's great army will be broken and he along with the false prophet, will be taken and cast alive into the lake of fire and brimstone. This will be their death sentence for all of eternity. And Revelation 20:1-3 explains the fate of their commander in chief:

And I saw an angel come down from heaven, having the key of the bottomless pit and a great chain in his hand. And he laid hold on the dragon, that old serpent, which is the Devil, and Satan, and bound him a thousand years, And cast him into the bottomless pit, and shut him up, and set a seal upon him, that he should deceive the nations no more, till the thousand years should be fulfilled...

Revelation 20:1-3

CHAPTER FIFTEEN

A DAY OF REST

In Hebrews 4:1-4, the Word of God exhorts the servants of God:

> *Let us therefore fear, lest, a promise being left us of entering into his rest, any of you should seem to come short of it. For unto us was the gospel preached, as well as unto them: but the word preached did not profit them, not being mixed with faith in them that heard it. For we which have believed do enter into rest, as he said, As I have sworn in my wrath, if they shall enter into my rest: although the works were finished from the foundation of the world. For he spake in a certain place of the seventh day on this wise, And God did rest the seventh day from all his works.*

God has left us a mighty promise. He promised the children of God that there will be a day of rest. The death of the Antichrist, the false prophet and the imprisonment of Satan will immediately usher in a glorious New Age on planet Earth, a dispensation of peace, health, and abundant prosperity such as the world has not known since Adam and Eve. Truly, it will be a glorious time. However, God warned us to have a Godly fear, because just as many of the children of Israel, who came out of bondage during the days of the Pharaohs of Egypt, fell short of the promise, the same could happen to us if we do not trust and cling to God's word.

The fourth verse brings out a profound truth. Do you realize that there was a period of time when Almighty God rested? Why? Why would God rest? When He created the world, He worked and labored for six days. Then He rested on the seventh day. God's resting on the seventh day was symbolic to something glorious; it was a figure of a wondrous event that will take place after Armageddon. God never does anything just to be doing it. There is a divine purpose behind everything He does. Let's look in Genesis and Exodus to bring some more light on the Scripture:

> *Thus the heavens and the Earth were finished, and all the host of them. And on the seventh day God ended his work which he had made; and he rested on the seventh day from all his work which he had made. And God blessed the seventh day, and sanctified it: because that in it he had rested from all his work which God created and made... For in six days the Lord made heaven and*

Earth, the sea, and all that in them is, and rested the seventh day: wherefore the Lord blessed the sabbath day, and hallowed it.

Genesis 2:1-3 and Exodus 20:11

That seventh day, after the creation of the Earth by God, was a special and blessed day (a day of rest). It was a sanctified, holy and consecrated day, a day which God set aside because He had ended all of His labor. Once again, God's resting on the seventh day after creation was symbolic of something wondrous to come. Let's examine Hebrews, the fourth chapter, a bit further.

There remaineth therefore a rest to the people of God. For he that is entered into his rest, he also hath ceased from his own works, as God did from his. Let us labour therefore to enter into that rest, lest any man fall after the same example of unbelief.

Hebrews 4:9-11

You might ask, "What are you trying to get across to us, Preacher? What is the point?" The main significance of the Sabbath Day of the Old Testament dispensation was much deeper than many religious people have comprehended down through the ages. The main significance of God's resting on the seventh day was to open up a divine revelation of what the whole world will someday experience. God was demonstrating to us that there is a divine day of rest coming to all those who will serve Him and endure to the end.

There is a day of rest coming, Beloved! We, who are saved, have been fighting and wrestling with demonic spirits night and day for many months and years. Sometimes we have been laughed at and made a mockery by unbelievers for our stand for God. We have been persecuted, buffed about, casting down evil imaginations and strong holds, and striving to make it. There have been much tribulations, fiery trials, fasting, praying and denial of self. But, through it all, we need not to worry, fret, nor be weary, for there is a day of rest coming!

These few verses of Scripture which we have read in Hebrews, are very important because they reveal to us just how close we are to the consummation of the ages. The Bible says, **"A day with the Lord is as a thousand years and a thousand years as one day."** (II Peter 3:8)

History reveals to us that from the time of God's creation of the world when Adam and Eve entered and until our present day, it has been well into six thousand years. And both Jews and Christian Biblical theologians agree that we are well into Day six. Therefore, mankind is very close to entering a new dispensation of God's calendar. We are near the threshold of entering the seventh day with God since Adam and Eve's Garden of Eden.

Beloved, you and I are privileged to be living in the season of the consummation of the ages: The very last hours of the sixth day. Six is the number of a man according to Revelation 13:18 and

Genesis 1:26-31. Seven is the number of God (which means consummation or complete). Now, what is the day of rest? The seventh day (this day of rest) will be the millennium reign or thousand-year reign (the seventh day of mankind since Adam's creation). It will be a thousand-year period, where the world will experience the most peaceful moments since the beginning of time.

After Armageddon, the death of the Antichrist, the false prophet and the imprisonment of Satan, Jesus Christ Himself will set up His throne in Jerusalem and He will be here on Earth to rule the world. His rulership will be an administration of true peace and prosperity. Satan will have been chained in the pit and will not be able to influence people to start wars or crimes. Apostle John wrote, Satan would be bound in this pit for a thousand years (Revelation 20:1-3) and this imprisonment will be the cause of the end of all wars.

Nebuchadnezzar's Image of Time

Nebuchadnezzar, King of Babylon, had a mighty vision one evening, which troubled and terrified him. This vision was "The Image of Time," and there was only one man in all of Babylon able to give the interpretation. His name was Daniel, the great Hebrew prophet.

The vision troubled the king so much that he called for all of the wise men and magicians in Babylon. He told them if they could interpret his dream, he would give them gifts, rewards and great honor. But, if they could not, he would have them cut into pieces. And the king made it even more difficult for them, saying he would not reveal what he saw in the dream. They would have to tell the king what he saw and also give the interpretation.

The wise men of Babylon told the king there is no man in all of Babylon able to do such a thing. Then, King Nebuchadnezzar went into a rage and sent out a decree to have all the wise men and magicians in Babylon killed and cut into pieces. Word got out to Daniel concerning the king's decree. Daniel asked for permission to come before the king. He told the king to "Give me some time in prayer... There is a God in Heaven who reveals secrets and the hidden things of darkness." He said, "My God will show me what you dreamed and give me the interpretation." Later, Daniel went back to make known the dream and the interpretation of Nebuchadnezzar's "Image of Time." The prophet Daniel begins to speak to the king. Let's read in Daniel 2:31-35:

> *Thou, O king, sawest, and behold a great image. This great image, whose brightness was excellent, stood before thee; and the form thereof was terrible. This image's head was of fine gold, his breast and his arms of silver, his belly and his thighs of brass. His legs of iron, his feet part of iron and part of clay. Thou sawest till that a stone was cut out without hands, which smote the*

image upon his feet that were of iron and clay, and brake them into pieces. Then was the iron, the clay, the brass, the silver, and the gold broken to pieces together, and became like the chaff of the summer threshingfloors; and the wind carried them away, that no place was found for them: and the stone that smote the image became a great mountain, and filled the whole Earth.

Daniel 2:31-34

Now the head of gold which the king saw in "The Image (statue) of Time" represented Nebuchadnezzar himself and his kingdom of ancient Babylon. It represented his kingdom's rise to world power in 606 B.C. and the fall. As you go down on this "Image of Time" to the chest and arms of silver, it represented the rise of the Medes and Persians who conquered Nebuchadnezzar's ancient Babylon in 536 B.C. As you move along further in history by going down further in "The Image of Time," the belly and thighs were made of brass. The brass represented the Greek Empire led by Alexander, The Great, who defeated the Medes and Persians around 330 B.C.

Moving along further in time, the legs of the image were made of iron and his feet was partly iron and partly clay. This represented the rise of the Ancient Roman Empire around 200 B.C. and its eventual demise in 476 A.D. and again in 1453 A.D. When the ancient Roman Empire fell the second time in 1453 A.D., it was broken up into several pieces and those pieces eventually became the nations of modern-day Europe as we know it today in our time.

Eventually, when he steps on the world stage, the Antichrist will revive the broken pieces of Ancient Rome (Europe) once again and start a diabolical world rulership as his predecessors did in the "Image of Time." His reign fulfills the prophecies of the Hebrew prophets of old and kicks off the tribulation period mentioned in the Book of Revelation.

Daniel went on to speak to King Nebuchadnezzar in verses 34-35. **"Thou sawest till a stone was cut without hands, which smote the image upon his feet that were iron and clay, and brake them to pieces. Then was the iron, the clay, the brass, the silver, and gold, broken to pieces together, and the wind carried them away that no place was found for them: and the stone that smote the image became a great mountain and filled the whole Earth."** Now this stone that will come and smite the **"Image of Time"** at its feet and cause the entire statue of nations from Babylon to the Antichrist's world empire during the seven-year tribulation period to crumble and collapse will be the Lord and Messiah, Jesus Christ.

This stone will come and smite the great image into tiny dust and the wind will blow the remains away and that stone will become a great mountain in the world. This stone, the Lord Jesus Christ, will make a dramatic and majestic return to Earth from Heaven with billions and billions of angels and the saints all riding on incredible white horses to crush the Antichrist and his hundreds of millions of soldiers in the valley of Armageddon ending the Antichrist's evil reign and all of his evil predecessors in the "Image of Time." This will kick off the beginning of a world with a thousand years of peace: **The Millennium Reign.**

Daniel went on to say in the 44th-45th verses:

> *And in the days of these kings (following Armageddon) shall the God of heaven set up a kingdom, which shall never be destroyed: And the kingdom shall not be left to other people (no more heathenistic world rulership) but it shall break into pieces and consume all those kingdoms and it (Jesus Christ's kingdom on Earth) shall stand forever. For as much as thou sawest that the stone was cut out of the mountain without hands, and that it broke into pieces the iron, the brass, the clay, the silver and gold; the great God hath made known to the king what shall come to pass hereafter: and the dream is certain and the interpretation thereof sure.*
>
> Daniel 2:44-45

In essence, through the mighty dream of the "Image of Time," Almighty God was revealing to king Nebuchadnezzar that the day is coming when the times of evil dictator's rulership of the Earth will abruptly come to an end. The "Image of Time" will crumble to dust and when that dust settles at the valley of Armageddon, the entire world will realize and recognize that the

185

Almighty Jesus Christ is Lord, and the incredible millennium reign will begin.

All of creation has been eagerly yearning for this day to come. Apostle Paul wrote:

> *For we know that the whole creation (the grass, flowers, trees, mountains, ground, animals, etc....) groaneth and travaileth in pain together until now. And not only they, but we also (mankind). Which have the first fruits of the spirit, even we ourselves groan within ourselves, waiting for the adoption, to wit, the redemption of our bodies.*
>
> **Romans 8:22-23**

Even creation can sense that deliverance for them is soon to come. They can sense that a day will come when there will be no more wars and violence. No more bombs dropped. No more bloodshed will be spilled, and they will not have to witness the horrors of crime, violence and wars. Therefore, they (the grass, flowers, trees, mountains, ground, animals) have been groaning in their own way in great expectation for the day of rest.

The Prophet Isaiah foresaw the creation's happiness after their groaning and travailing period was ended.

> *The Lord hath broken the staff of the wicked, and the sceptre of the rulers (at Armageddon). He who smote the people in wrath with a continual stroke, he (the Antichrist) that ruled the nations in anger, is persecuted*

and none hindereth (his destruction). The whole Earth is at rest, and is quiet: They (the creation) break forth into singing. Yea, the fir trees rejoice at thee (Jesus), and the cedars of Lebanon, saying since thou hast laid down, (come to the Earth) no feller is come up against us.

Isaiah 14:5-8

This will be the reaction and great delight of creation when the Antichrist is destroyed with all of his war machines and the Messiah brings His peace throughout the Earth.

Now that's the grass, trees, plants, and mountain's reaction to the glorious day of rest. Let's look at the animal's reaction to the ushering in of the millennium.

The wolf also shall dwell with the lamb, and the leopard shall lie down with the kid (goat): And the calf and young lion and fatling together; and a little child shall lead them. And the cow and bear shall feed; their young ones shall lie down together; and the lion shall eat straw like the ox. And the sucking child shall play on the hole of the asp (deadly snake). The weaned child shall put his hand on the cockatrice den (deadly serpent). They shall not hurt nor destroy in all my holy mountain: For the Earth shall be full of the knowledge of the Lord, as the waters cover the sea. And in that day (millennium reign) there shall be a root of Jesse (Jesus Christ) which shall

187

> *stand for an ensign of the people; to it shall the Gentiles*
> *seek: And his rest (the millennium) shall be glorious.*
>
> **Isaiah 11:6-10**

Isaiah is showing us that the animals will be delighted, also, during this thousand-year period, all of the animals in the world will, similar to humans, be at peace and harmony. Can you imagine a deadly wolf laying down next to a lamb, a leopard lying next to a little goat, and a lion and a calf together with no blood being shed at all? Can you picture these animals being kind and peaceful together? Can you picture a cow and bear being kind to each other and their young ones playing with each other? A mother telling her little child to "Go out and play with your snake and serpent pets, Sweetie." During this time, children will actually do this with no fear. None of the animals and wild beasts will fight nor devour each other, but they will have a nature to eat straw and grass instead of flesh. God said, "They (the wild beast) shall not hurt nor destroy in all my holy mountain." What a glorious time this will be!

Did you know that in Eden, during the days of Adam and Eve, before they sinned, peace was the original nature of animals? Back then, God gave the animal world a kind and peaceful nature. That's why Adam and Eve were able to live with those beasts with no fear of being hurt. Back then, at the beginning of creation, none in the animal world was carnivorous. All of the animals and beasts had a nature of eating the straw, leaves, and the grass of the Earth. But when Adam and Eve sinned, their disobedience not only corrupted the nature of mankind, but also the nature of the animal world. Not only did man begin to have dislike and violence toward one another, but also many animals had that same violent nature. You don't hear this mentioned often, but it's true: The sin of Adam and Eve affected the animal world, also.

The cats began to dislike the mice and dogs began to dislike the cats. The leopard began to devour almost any creature that strayed into his path. The birds began to hunt for and devour worms. The shark would begin to violently tear fish apart in the great seas. This has been the state of the animal world ever since: kill and devour or be killed and devoured. But, oh! When the millennium reign comes! The animals will once again live together in peace. This is exactly what Paul was talking about when he wrote, **"The whole creation groaneth."** They are in great anticipation of what's to come. These animals can sense it won't be much longer and their travail and sufferings as a result of the curse of sin will be all over. Jesus will be here living on Earth in person to see to it that there is peace in the world.

As stated earlier in this chapter, there will be no war on Earth during this time. For all nations will be taught of Jesus Christ, Himself, and will walk in His path:

The word that Isaiah the son of Amoz saw concerning Judah and Jerusalem. And it shall come to pass in the last days, that the mountain of the LORD'S house shall be established in the top of the mountains, and shall be exalted above the hills; and all nations shall flow unto it. And many people shall go and say, Come ye, and let us go up to the mountain of the Lord, to the house of the God of Jacob; and he will teach us of his ways, and we will walk in his paths: for out of Zion shall go forth the law, and the Word of the Lord from Jerusalem. And He (Jesus) shall judge among the nations; and they shall beat their swords into plowshares, and their spears into pruninghooks: nations shall not lift up sword against nation, neither shall they learn war any more.

Isaiah 2:1-4

But in the last days it shall come to pass, that the mountain of the house of the Lord shall be established in the top of the mountains, and it shall be exalted above the hills; and people shall flow unto it. And many nations shall come, and say, Come, and let us go up to the mountain of the Lord, and to the house of the God of Jacob; and he will teach us of his ways, and we will walk in his paths: for the law shall go forth of Zion, and the Word of the Lord from Jerusalem. And He (Jesus) shall judge among many people, and rebuke strong nations afar off; and they shall beat their swords into plowshares, and their spears into pruninghooks: nation shall not lift up a sword (weapon) against nation, neither shall they learn war any more. But they shall sit every man under his vine and under his fig tree; and none shall make them afraid: for the mouth of the Lord of hosts hath spoken it.

Micah 4:1-4

This mountain of God (The little stone that will smite King Nebuchadnezzar's "Image of Time" into tiny fragments of dust and the wind will blow away)! And the little stone will become a great mountain in the city of Jerusalem, towering majestically in the land of Israel as a great beacon of light for the nations of the four corners of the Earth.

Oh, This mountain of God! There will not be enough words in a million dictionaries to completely describe its beauty. And at the high summit will lie the Holy temple and the throne of the King of kings and Lord of lords, the Messiah, Jesus Christ, clothed in all of His royal apparel. And all of the nations of the world will come year after year to give Him homage, hear a word from the Master, and bow down in worship of Him. And this stone, this great stone, which the builders rejected shall become the head of the corner. And yes, every knee will ultimately bow and tongue confess that this "Great Stone," Jesus Christ, is Lord!

Jesus Christ will have to rebuke many nations because of their possession of weapons which they used in times past. The Lord will make these nations transform all of their weapons into industrial tools. And no more money will be spent by these

191

nations for war machines causing not only peace on the Earth but great prosperity, for the trillions of dollars spent for war in times past will be spent for the needs of the people instead. The people of the nations will come up often to visit the Lord in Jerusalem, which will be the new world capital. They will sit at the feet of Jesus to receive instructions of His ways that they may learn how to walk in His path.

Oh, what a day this will be! The Bible tells us in Isaiah that there will be no more infant of days, nor an old man that will not fill his days. In other words, no one will die young; no one will die prematurely, for there will be no sickness nor disease on the Earth. People who survived the tribulation period and entered the millennium will eventually experience death because they will yet have a mortal body. However, there will be none that die through sickness and disease like now; they will live long and healthy lives.

During that time, if a person died at one hundred, for instance, that will be considered a short life. It will be common for one to live for several hundred years. There will yet be unbelievers and sinners on the Earth, and God will at times have to chasten them for their disobedience. People will greatly prosper, building beautiful homes, planting crops in abundance and their labors in the Earth will not be in vain. Read Isaiah 65:20-25 for reference.

Before the rapture, Jesus had made a promise to the church: He said, **"And he that overcometh, and keepeth my works unto the end, to him will I give power over the nations: And he shall rule them..."** (Revelation 2:26-27). Jesus also promised us one day, we will rule over cities on the Earth. Some will rule over five cities and some will rule over as many as ten cities. The Apostle John saw this promise of authority to the church being fulfilled during the millennium reign in his vision while on Patmos. He wrote:

> *And I saw thrones, and they sat upon them (the saints who made the rapture and came back to Earth with Jesus), and judgement (authority, rulership) was given unto them: and I saw the souls of them that were beheaded for the witness of Jesus (those saved and murdered during the tribulation period), and for the Word of God, and which had not worshipped the beast, neither his image, neither had received his mark upon their foreheads, or in their hands; and they lived and reigned with Christ a thousand years.*
>
> Revelation 20:4

What John saw here was the reward for those who made the rapture and those who refused to follow the Antichrist's policy during the tribulation accepting Christ by faith and were slain by the Antichrist as a result. These people will be sitting on their own thrones in Jerusalem, along with Jesus, during the millennium and will rule on the Earth with Him. Jerusalem will be to the entire world what Washington D.C. is to America: The capital where the chief leaders and lawmakers dwell. From there, we will be given the authority by Christ to judge the towns, cities, and nations of the world as governors, mayors, presidents and kings. **"Do ye not know that the saints shall judge (rule) the world?"** (1 Corinthians 6:2) **"Blessed and holy is he that hath part in the first resurrection: on such the second death hath no power, but they shall be priests of God and of Christ, and shall reign with him a thousand (millennium) years."** (Revelation 20:6) For further study on this great day of rest: The millennium reign, study Zachariah 14:8-21, Zachariah 8:21-22, Isaiah 66:23, Isaiah 33:24, Daniel 2:44-45, St. Luke 19:11-19 and St. Matthew 25:21.

CHAPTER SIXTEEN

ONE LAST WAR

⸙

For many years I have heard several individuals speak of Armageddon as being the last war on Earth, but technically, this is not true according to the Scriptures. According to the Book of Revelation, there will yet be one more war the Earth must endure in history one thousand years after the battle of Armageddon.

In the Book of Revelation, you will recall the passage of Scripture where it said that Satan will be taken by an angel, chained and cast into the bottomless pit for a thousand years, a place where he won't be able to influence the minds and hearts of people. This will be the main reason why there will be peace on Earth and no wars during that span of time. However, this will not be the end of the devil, for Revelation 20:3 states: "**And after that he must be loosed a little season.**"

He will be loosed from his great chain and shackle, which had him bound in the pit for a thousand years and will be set free.

And guess what? You guessed it. He will immediately stir up trouble once again in the Earth, which had nothing but peace and harmony for a millennium. **"And when the thousand years are expired, Satan shall be loosed out of his prison. And shall go out to deceive the nations which are in the four quarters of the Earth, Gog and Magog, to gather them together to battle: the number of whom is as the sand of the sea."** (Revelation 20:7-8)

There are a few things about end-time prophecy where many theologians have had some questions and differences of opinions. This is one of them and I want to address this. The words Gog and Magog are also mentioned in Ezekiel the 38th chapter concerning the nation of Russia's failed invasion attempt of Israel, which was extensively addressed earlier in Chapter 11. I stated that it is believed this event will take place just prior to or shortly following the rapture at the beginning of the seven-year tribulation period. This Gog and Magog mentioned here at the end of the millennium reign is not the same event mentioned in Ezekiel the 38th and 39th chapters. That invasion attempt by Russia and its allies will come from the North downward to Israel according to the prophecy. However, the invasion attempt mentioned in Revelation 20:7-9 will come from the four corners of the Earth. The attackers, after the millennium, will come from everywhere on the Earth toward the land of Israel. Can you see the difference? So, this is a totally different invasion from the one in Ezekiel the 38th and 39th chapters. This invasion in Revelation the 20th chapter will take place a little over one thousand years later.

Can you imagine this after all those hundreds of years in prison? Almost as soon as the devil is released, he works up enough deception in the four corners of the world to assemble an army as large as the sand of the seashore. In a short period of time, he will stir a great multitude, possibly more than the battle of Armageddon, to follow him.

This multitude that will join Satan will not be all nations but many nations of people who lived in peace during the millennium. These people, in their hearts, didn't like the idea of following the concepts and laws of Jesus Christ. These are those who Christ will have to rebuke often during the thousand-year reign. (Zechariah 14:16-19, Isaiah 2:4, and Ezekiel 29:9-14)

The question is, where will this massive multitude of soldiers assembled by Satan be headed? And what will they be seeking to do? Satan will assemble them to attack and destroy Jesus and the saints in the world capital of Jerusalem. He will somehow convince this multitude in the world that we are their enemies and must be destroyed. This will literally be Satan and his evil principality's last try to destroy God and rule the universe. It will be the very last war of history. However, it will end swiftly as we read Revelation 20:9-10:

And they (Satan and his multitude) went up on the breadth of the Earth, and compassed (surrounded) the camp of the saints about, and the beloved city: and fire came down from God out of heaven, and devoured them. And the devil that deceived them was cast into the lake of fire and brimstone, where the beast and the false prophet are, and shall be tormented day and night for ever and ever.

This, Beloved, will be the complete end of Satan. He will be destroyed. And as the prophet Ezekiel put it, **"Never shalt thou be any more."** (Ezekiel 28:19)

Immediately after this, the great judgement will begin for those who died unbelievers; these are those who refused to repent of their sins and turn from evil. Those who died in this state and were in the prison of Hell prior to the rapture will be resurrected and standing before a great white throne where the Almighty God will be seated.

There will be billions and billions of souls standing there. The murderer will be there. Men and women who left the natural uses of their bodies will be there (men with men and women with women sexually). Robbers and thieves will be there. The prostitute, gangster, drug addict, and those who embrace pornography will attend. The male and female strippers will stand there. Those who hate and despise people because of the color of their skin will be there also. Those women and men who believed in and engaged in killing unborn babies will stand there. Those children who were rebellious and disrespectful toward their parents will be there. The drunkard will be there. Those who while they lived, made a mockery of Christians and their worship services will be there. Those who hung around the church and their services but never believed nor surrendered their lives to God will be there. Those who were once saved but backslid and did not get back to God before they died will be there. Great men and women will be there. Kings, presidents, rulers of the past, great entertainers, great businessmen and women, the educated, rich and poor of all nationalities, races and creeds will be there. They will stand there if while they lived, they did not repent of their sins, turn away from their evil lifestyles, and accept Jesus Christ as their Lord and Savior. (Read Hebrews 9:27, Ecclesiastes 12:13-14, and St. John 5:28-29 for further study) In the Book of Romans of the New Testament, Paul describes these sins in Romans 1:16-32.

The Bible says, as they stand before the Chief Judge of the universe (the Lord God), the Bible will be opened and the Book of Life (which contains all the names of those who were true servants of God). The Bible says, and those people who will stand there will be judged by the Bible according to their works while they lived, and then the angel of God will be asked to search the Book of Life and see if any of these people's names are written therein. The Word of God then tells us, "And whosoever was not found written in this Book of Life was then

cast into the lake of fire where the devil, Antichrist, and the false prophet are and shall be tormented with them for ever and ever."
Read Revelation 20:11-15.

CHAPTER SEVENTEEN

A NEW HEAVEN
AND EARTH

———————————ꙄꙆꙄ———————————

A fter judgement day, God will burn the entire Earth with fire to purify it from all of the evil that took place since Eden. (II Peter 3:10) He will burn it, but not destroy it. Note: Those who were saved during the tribulation period and survived and those who were saved during the millennium will not be harmed by this purging of the Earth. Immediately afterward will follow the beginning of the new and everlasting age where there will be a new Heaven and Earth. This will be an age where there will never again be any evil. An age where there will never again be a devil, antichrist or false prophets. An age where no one will ever die: For death will be destroyed for ever and ever. It will be an age where no one will ever know what it is to be sick or in pain. For all demonic spirits will have been cast into the lake of fire and never to be set free again. Everyone living in this age will be happy and walking about the Earth with joy unspeakable and full of glory. Oh, what a wonderful time this will be! As great as the millennium was, it will not, in any wise, compare to this new age. The millennium will be like the salad bar or appetizer to the main course.

Apostle John summed this up best in his vision in Revelation the 21st chapter. He wrote:

> *And I saw a new heaven and a new Earth: for the first heaven and the first Earth were passed away (Also, read II Peter 3:10 and Hebrews 1:10-12); and there was no more sea. And I John saw the holy city, new Jerusalem, coming down from God out of heaven, prepared as a bride adorned for her husband. And I heard a great voice out of heaven saying, Behold, the tabernacle of God is with men, and he will dwell with them, and they shall be his people, and God himself shall be with them, and be their God (Jehovah, Jesus, and the Holy Spirit also known as the Holy Trinity). And God shall wipe away all tears from their eyes; and there shall be no more death, neither sorrow, nor crying, neither shall there be any more pain: for the former things are passed away. And he (God) that sat upon the throne said, Behold, I make all things new...*

Revelation 21:1-5

Apostle John saw this new kingdom of Heaven and Earth. He saw that the first Heaven and Earth were done away with. God told John, "Look, I have made everything new." Everything new in the Heaven and in the Earth. This age will be a brand-new fresh beginning for all of the universe. John also saw in Heaven, New Jerusalem, the Holy City of God, descending to the Earth from Heaven to replace the old city. This great city had been in Heaven for thousands of years, waiting for this glorious moment to come. This is the place Jesus was talking about when He said:

Let not your heart be troubled: ye believe in God, believe also in me. In my Father's house are many mansions: if it were not so, I would have told you. I go to prepare a place for you. And if I go and prepare a place for you, I will come again, and receive you unto myself; that where I am, there ye may be also.

St. John 14:1-3

The new city (this glorious eternal city), New Jerusalem, will come down to the new Earth from Heaven and will be that place which Christ has prepared for you and I who are alive in that day. It will be the greatest city ever known to man. For Christ, Himself, would be the architect and master builder. Inside of this city will be those many mansions which Jesus promised us. These mansions will make the ones on this present Earth look like ghetto slums. Truly, when we see them and walk into them, we will be able to fully grasp what the Word of God said in I Corinthians 2:9: "But as it is written eye hath not seen, nor ear heard, neither have entered into the heart of man, the things which God hath prepared for them that love him." The Bible also states, "He (or she) that overcometh shall inherit all things." (Revelation 21:7) Those of us who refused to bow to Satan's wickedness and sinful lifestyles, giving our hearts to Jesus Christ and earnestly seeking to walk in His ways, will be those who will walk into and reside in this city forever.

As you examine further in Revelation, the 20th Chapter, you will find that an angel came and carried up John into a great mountain in the new Earth. And from there, he saw the New Jerusalem once again descending to the Earth out of Heaven. John described this city as one whose light was the glory of God. This glory, which will shine throughout the city, was like the shining of a precious jasper stone, clear as crystal.

John said the city had a high wall around it and twelve gates: three on the west, three on the east, three on the south and three on the north ends. These twelve gates, which will be made of pure pearls and will have the names of the twelve tribes of the children of Israel engraved in them. The wall of this great new city will have twelve foundations and the names of the twelve Apostles of Christ written on it. The foundations of the city's walls will be garnished with several precious stones: the jasper, sapphire, chalcedony, emerald, sardonyx, sarius, chrysolite, beryl, topaz, chrysoprasus, jacinth and the amethyst. I can't imagine that there are enough words in the English dictionary to describe how beautiful the outside walls, foundation, and gates of this city will look like. And we haven't even talked in depth about the inside as of yet.

Entering into this eternal city, one will find that all the streets are paved with a gold that is so pure it is transparent. God sure does know how to entertain guests, doesn't He? Can you imagine walking around in an extremely large city where every step you take on the streets will be on pure transparent gold? John wrote that this city will not need the light from the sun, moon, nor stars. For God's glory will be its eternal light.

Now, you should know that outside of New Jerusalem there will be a daytime and nighttime. The sun will rise in the morning and light the Earth during the day and when it goes down, there will be night just at it is in the present day. There will always be day and night. There will always be a sun, moon, and stars. And there will always be the changing of seasons, even during this new age. (Read Genesis 8:22, Psalms 89:34-37 and Jeremiah 31:35-36) The sun, moon, stars and changing of season is an eternal ordinance of God that will never end. During this new age, the only place on Earth where this ordinance will not be in operation will be within the new city which descended to Earth from Heaven. For God, Himself will live in there and His presence and glory will be the sun, moon and stars of the city. Those who live in this city will be the saints who were caught up in the rapture and those who turned to God during the tribulation period and were slain by the Antichrist. These saints will have special positions in this new kingdom. They will live in New Jerusalem with Christ and rule the four corners of the Earth as they did during the millennium reign. Each of them will have a mansion in this city and will be able to go in and out of the city anytime they choose. I believe the New Jerusalem will be much, much bigger than the current Jerusalem in order to accommodate all of the saints of the rapture and those who were persecuted and killed during the tribulation period but made it to Glory. In fact, I believe the entire Earth will be much, much bigger than the current Earth because of John's vision in Revelation 21:1 where he mentioned he saw a new Heaven and Earth where there was no more sea. Here are some interesting statistics. According to the U.S. Geology Survey, about seventy-one percent of Earth is water (only twenty-nine percent is land) and of that seventy-one percent of water, ninety-six and a half percent is the saline water contained in the ocean. The remaining three and a half percent is drinking water from lakes, rivers, and so forth. Because John recorded that this ninety-six and a half percent of ocean water will be no more, can you imagine how much additional dry land will be available? This is why I believe the Earth will be much larger; there will be much more land available for us to tread on. The saints will have a powerful, immortal body like unto angels (including the abilities to fly) and I personally believe we will be able to recognize each other as we did before the rapture. However, we will not marry nor be given in marriage according to St. Matthew 22:29-30.

On the outside of New Jerusalem, all over the new world, will live those people who survived the tribulation period and entered the millennium along with those who were born from them. They will be those who refused to join Satan's army in that last attempt to destroy God and the saints. (Revelation 20:7-10) These people will live in the new age. They will also have bodies that cannot die, and they will live forever in the new world with great joy, peace and happiness. However, they will be a little lower in authority and glory than those who live in New Jerusalem with God Almighty.

> *And the nations of them which are saved shall walk in the light (glory) of it: and the kings of the Earth do bring their glory and honor into it. And the gates of it shall not be shut at all by day: For there shall be no night there. And they shall bring the glory and honor of the nations into it. And there shall in no wise enter into it anything that defileth, neither whatsoever worketh abomination, or maketh a lie: But they which are written in the lambs Book of Life.*
>
> **Revelation 21:24-27**

The new kingdom of Earth will have nations all over the world like this present one with cities, towns, and homes. There will be those who will govern regions of the Earth, but they will govern in righteousness and holiness. There will be no evil anywhere in the new Earth. We, who will be in New Jerusalem, will rule over different areas of the world as during the millennium. New Jerusalem will be as the old Jerusalem during the millennium reign, the capital of the new world. And the Almighty God will be there with us to oversee everything. What a great plan of salvation this is, Beloved.

John wrote that these nations of the world and their kings will periodically come to visit the eternal city to pay tribute to it and the Everlasting God. And the Bible says there will be none that will enter this pure city that is unclean. For all over the world, there will be none who are not saved and sealed with the righteousness of God. And it will be impossible for sin and evil to surface in the world again. For further description on the new Jerusalem, read Revelation the 21st chapter.

CHAPTER EIGHTEEN

BELOVED, WHAT MANNER OF PERSONS OUGHT YE TO BE?

⎯⎯⎯⎯⎯⎯⎯⎯⎯⎯ ୬୧୬୧ ⎯⎯⎯⎯⎯⎯⎯⎯⎯⎯

The mystery of iniquity doth already work, only He who now letteth will let until He be taken out of the way. (II Thessalonians 2:7) Consider our present-day here within the early decades of the twenty-first century and perhaps the season where the rapture could occur. Perhaps it is the very season where the sinister Antichrist will be revealed in the Earth and come forth to begin his reign of terror, ushering in the great tribulation period, which will be the most devastating period of time mankind has ever known.

Has my writing persuaded you that the Lord is soon to come? Or are you one of those who are skeptical if there will be a rapture, tribulation period, and day of judgement?

Apostle Peter wrote that in the last days, there would be mockers and ridiculers walking after their own unlawful desires. They will make fun of Christianity as they boldly and foolishly continue to live an ungodly lifestyle. They will have smirks on their faces as they say, "Where is the promise of His coming? Where is your Jesus? You mean He hasn't come yet? When is your so-called rapture going to happen? Where are your so-called judgements of the Book of Revelation? Ever since our fathers fell asleep, many centuries ago, the world continues to exist as usual."

Peter is quick to remind these foolish kinds of people that this is a state of mind that many had in the days of Noah. They were happy-go-lucky, living in sin with no fear of God and His word. Noah kept warning them that judgement was coming, but they laughed at him and despised him. God opened up the heavens and poured out great rain, which destroyed everyone living except Noah and his family. For they believed God's word. Christ told us:

> *As the days of Noah were, so shall also the coming of the son of man (Jesus) be. For as in the days that were before the flood they were eating and drinking, marrying and given in marriage, until the day that Noah entered into the ark, and knew not until the flood came, and took them all away; so shall also the coming of the son of man be.*
>
> St. Matthew 24:37-39

Peter wrote:

> *Whereby the world that then was, being overflowed with water, perished: But the heavens and the Earth, which are now, by the same word are kept in store, reserved unto fire against the day of judgement and perdition (destruction) of ungodly men... The Lord is not slack (slothful) concerning his promise (of the judgement day) as some men count slackness; but is long suffering to us-ward, not willing (desiring) that any should perish, but that all should come to repentance. But the day of the Lord (the tribulation period) will come as a thief in the night; in which the heavens shall pass away with a great noise, and the elements shall melt with fervent heat, the Earth also and the works that are therein shall be burned up. Seeing then that all these things shall be dissolved, what manner of persons ought ye to be in all holy conversation (lifestyles) and godliness, looking for and hastening (quickly preparing yourself) unto the coming of the day of God.*

II Peter 3:6-12

Peter is warning the unbelievers that, while you are not preparing for the rapture, the Lord's day will sneak up on you as a thief in the night and then it will be too late. He revealed to us that when this day of the Lord comes, it will be so devastating until even the elements of the atmosphere will melt with fervent heat. The Earth will also be on fire under the wrath of God's judgements. Peter said, seeing then that all this trouble is coming as promised by God's word; **What manner of person ought you be** in getting your life right with your maker that these great destructions don't fall upon you?

Beloved, I believe this book has touched your heart. I believe that your life, after reading this book, will never be the same. You did not pick up and read this book by chance. It was the divine purpose of God. I want to pray a fervent prayer for you right now. If you are not right with God and if you do not know Jesus in the forgiveness of your sins and therefore not ready for the rapture when it comes, repeat these important words to the Lord.

Prayer of Confession

Say, "Lord Jesus, I confess that I am a sinner and I do not know You in the forgiveness of my sins. And if You came today, I would not be ready. Lord Jesus, after reading this book, my heart has been touched. I want to be saved. I want to be right. I want to turn from a life of sin forever. I want to be set free from the evil shackles of Satan. Lord Jesus, You said, if we shall confess with our mouth, the Lord Jesus and believe in our heart that God has raised You from the dead, we shall be delivered. Lord Jesus, this day I confess with my mouth that You are Lord and I renounce every aspect of my former life that I embraced, which was contrary to Your Holy Word. Lord Jesus, come into my heart, wash me, cleanse me and live within my heart forever and ever!"

Oh, praise God! Glory to God! Just worship Him, my dear friend; give your Savior praise and worship. Let Him minister to you right now where you are. He's there with you and He has heard your sincere prayer. You will never ever be the same! Lift your hand to Him in praise and worship and let Him saturate you.

Right now, your sins are forgiven, my dear friend. You don't have to yield to sin anymore. You are now a son of the Most High God, and an heir to sit on a throne in the eternal city with the God of Heaven and all of His congregation of saints. We must diligently serve him, Beloved, waiting for His soon return.

Now, therefore, let us go forth, spread the good news and tell the story! "Go tell it on the mountains, over the hills and everywhere!" Tell it in the churches. Let it be known in our schools. Tell it in the marketplaces. Proclaim this in the valleys and declare it in the highways, hedges and lanes of our cities. Compel them, my friends! Enlighten those of all walks of life, both the white-collar and the blue-collar workers. Tell the drug addict, the harlot, the alcoholic, and the agnostic. Tell the adolescent, as well as the adult. Inform the athletes, comedians, movie actors and actresses, the rock, pop, jazz, country, and blues singers. Tell the white man, the black man, both Jew and Gentile. Tell the rich and the poor. Tell the imprisoned and the free. Tell them our majestic Jesus is coming soon! And meanwhile, as we are waiting, always remember the words of our Lord, when He warned us to "Take heed to ourselves that our hearts are not overcharged with the cares of this life so that day does not catch us unprepared."

Now, therefore, I compel you, my friends, by the divine inspiration of the Holy Spirit of God, "Beware!" Be prayerful and be diligent. Be watchful and be earnest in your devotion to God. Be always mindful that somewhere in the Earth, lurking within the cracks, crevices and dark shadows prowls a diabolical Antichrist: "The Mystery of Iniquity," who is already diligently at work.

Let us pray

Heavenly Father, I pray for all of those who have taken the time to read and study this important publication. I pray that You will open the eyes of those that have been closed to the abundant truth of Your Holy Word. Stir those who have been out of the ark of safety to lay down the evil things of this world and begin to earnestly follow You with all of their hearts. Stir them to daily pray and read Your word. Stir them to faithfully attend a Holy Spirit-filled church where the anointing of God abides. Stir them to let go of anything that is not like You. I pray this in the powerful name of Jesus. Amen.

ABOUT THE AUTHOR

R ichard Glenn was an outstanding baseball player in the Detroit, Michigan area as a youngster. His ultimate dream was to become a great major league baseball player. Extremely dedicated to the cause, he ate, slept and dreamed this national pastime. Richard Glenn's  team, Detroit Edison Post, won three championships in American Legion baseball: the Detroit City title, the State of Michigan title and the prestigious Kentucky Tournament in Ashland, Kentucky, all in the summer of 1970. Richard led the American Legion in hitting (386 average), doubles, hits and runs scored. But, in the summer of 1970, while inching closer to his ultimate goal, he heard a divine call from the Almighty God. He was convinced there was another purpose for his life. He abruptly and astonishingly, to many, turned from his beloved sandlots to take heed to that divine call into a journey in life to hit singles, doubles, home runs, dazzling throws and catches for the master, Jesus Christ. Dedicating his life to that call faithfully for over forty years, he has witnessed the Gospel of our Lord, Jesus Christ, through his literature and preaching. Through the years, multitudes have been touched and inspired by his distinct and simplified style of teaching. May the good Lord inspire you also through this classic book.

Contact Us

To order books and audio from this ministry, please visit:

www.richardglennministries.com

Please leave your comments and prayer requests on the website or contact us by email at info@richardglennministries.com.

Audio and video formats are available, including a 10-part series of this study with twelve hours of lecturing on the topic. Please visit the website or:

Social Media

RichardGlennMinistries

eBook & Audio Book formats available

Booking

To book Richard Glenn for speaking and events contact:

Richard Glenn Ministries

Email: info@richardglennministries.com

P.O. Box 442073 Detroit, MI 48244